Women Call — Men Respond

Secrets of Passion and Pleasure

Women Call — Men Respond

Secrets of Passion and Pleasure

By
Maureen McDonough
and
James Rutherford

HarperCollins*Publishers New Zealand*

First published 1995
HarperCollinsPublishers (New Zealand) Limited
P.O. Box 1, Auckland

ISBN 1 86950 160 8

Typeset and designed by Pages Literary Pursuits
Printed by HarperCollins Hong Kong

Contents

Dedication and Acknowledgements

Maureen

To the memory of Tom Barry, my father and the first man in my life, who always admired, respected and protected my spirit.

I wish to acknowledge my parents, Esther and Tom, for their love and vision for their children. Also Pat, Joan and David for enduring this spoiled child. To Bill, Trevor, Tania, Lara and Lehua for teaching me to be a wife and mother. To Mitsue Cook Carlson for pestering me to write. And to Geoffrey, my night coach, and my knight in armour.

James

To April, my source, my creative light, my friend; I hold you preciously in my heart and heroically in my life.

I wish to acknowledge Don Sturtevant, who taught me pride in my writing and mind, and Dave and Sherry Pettus, whose brilliance permeates both their teachings and their example. Mostly, I wish to acknowledge Reid, Rachel, Judy and Robert whose highest expression of love has always been their exceptional good humour.

Maureen and James

Both of us also wish to acknowledge our many readers, men and women, who have been as midwives to the birth of this child, and to our many friends who have cheered us on.

Most importantly, we offer our sincere gratitude for the genius, the sensitivity and the insight of Dr Victor Baranco.

If you would like information about seminars and tapes, send enquiries to International Seminars, 737 Bishop Street, Suite #2850, Honolulu, HI, 96813, or fax 808-538-7219.

Preface

There is a new current of thought, feeling and power emerging in the world. Women everywhere feel it. It cuts through belief systems, religions, nations and cultures. At the same time, it is not out to prove anything; it is not beating a drum. Instead, it is motivated by its own discoveries of truth. It reaches to the roots of what it means to be human, to the depths of inspiration, magic, natural motivation and sensuality. This current is all about the *juice* in human relationships — what really turns women on, what really turns men on. Women have been pushed so far into the denial of themselves that they are now emerging, as if from a war, into a realisation that they can truly have it all. They can have their individuality, and they can also have their men happy and turned on. This movement nurtures everyone — children, the elderly, women and men. It isn't feminism. It is *Womanism.*

Chapter 1

Setting the Stage

Maureen: *The heart of you*

A friend recently completed a three-day workshop on how to date successfully in the 90s. She called me afterwards and spent thirty excited minutes describing how much fun she'd had, and how many things she'd learned. I listened patiently while she related tips on things like personal grooming and places to meet men. And then she told how class members gave each other feedback on one another's clothes, speech, presentation and so on. It did sound fun, actually. And cute. Unfortunately, it had nothing to do with man-woman sensuality and relationships. Because if a woman knows how to turn up the dials to get what she wants, she won't even have to brush her teeth. The men will be there; and they will be the right men at the right time.

No seminar will tell you what we're going to tell you. No psychologist will, either. Only a handful of sex experts can tell you what you will find in this book. You have never read a book like this one — it is based on the most advanced research available. This is the only material about men and women which doesn't bore me to tears, the only material which has given me a spin that lasts a lifetime. In every class I sponsor, I disclose only what has worked for me. I talk only from my gut experience. And I have never found anything so profoundly accurate about men and women as the information you are about to receive. What you are about to read is the *heart* of man-woman.

However, when I first heard this information I was distrustful. I remember thinking it was another way to subjugate women.

1

At other times, it just sounded bizarre. But since then, I have been amazed. You, too, may experience different reactions when you first hear this information. It cuts quickly to the crux of the matter. Yet finally, this book will call you to a new level of naturalness in your relationships that has rung true and clear every single day of my life.

Your life will change for the better after reading this book. Fortunately, you will not be "jacked up and glazed over" with some kind of quick fix. Instead, you will discover honest-to-goodness power. This information has what I call truthful beauty — knowledge that stays with you and blooms repeatedly in your life and relationships. It speaks to you because it speaks to the truth, the heart, in you.

James: *A new way*

I was dumped into my adolescence in the late 60s. Because I grew up in a household with a feminist mother and sister, the oppression of women was an issue that was woven into my entire concept of sexuality ... along with, of course, getting to second-base with a girl. But women were complaining then — and boy, was I listening! As a result, I became convinced I was a new man for the times, or something — a better man, a more understanding man. Maybe I was. Or maybe the great wave of the sixties had just left me mucking around in its backwash.

In any case, in my limited way, I took on the cause. I remember writing some high school papers on feminism, and challenging my teachers with feminist ideas — I was a new feminist kind of guy. Then one day, my best friend's mother fouled it up. She asked me why I thought I was different when I was just providing what the women in my life wanted, exactly like the other millions of men throughout history. I didn't understand her at first. In fact, I'm sure I argued with her. But then I realised I was just trying to be my mother's and sister's hero — trying to be the white knight, like all those men before me.

It was many years later that my fiancée (now wife) and I began to research man-woman sensuality. As a result of our study, we have come to a profound new understanding of man-woman dynamics, as well as to a new ease and acceptance about our natural responses to each other. A great deal has fallen into place for us — not because we feel we have been given some set of "right answers", but because every day we continue to discover right questions.

Of course, we still have our issues from time to time, but these no longer seem to centre around what was, before, a fundamental ignorance about men and women. Instead, we have the feeling that a war has ended, that a world of confusion and uncertainty has left us forever. We are experiencing a new sense of freedom and confidence together. Even better, we're having fun. It is our intention that these principles open up the same sense of possibility, freedom and fun for you and your man.

Chapter 2

The Road Less Travelled

Where you find out if you are able to choose pleasure

. . . He kept his arms entwined about her, and his hands remained pressed into the soft curvature of her back. Instead of touching her or stroking her, he caressed her with his eyes. "You're sure … this time?"

"Absolutely sure." All her senses were focused on one need now; she desired nothing beyond what Glenn could give her. "I've never been so sure of anything in my life … ."

After their mouths met, only to part for an instant before coming together again, they slowly drifted toward the other room. They stopped once, to hold each other in a blind, almost fierce embrace. The kiss that followed lacked the sweetness and softness of their previous kisses; an urgency gripped both of them now. At first her palms had brushed across his shoulders and back, but soon her fingers were digging deeply into the taut, tense muscles which contracted and flexed rapidly, almost violently. He startled her when he broke free of her arms, but it was only to lift her, with a marvellous lightness, off her feet. She buried her head in the hollow of his shoulder as he carried her into the bedroom.

She closed her eyes and kept them closed until he laid her tenderly on the bed. Her lids fluttered open when she sensed him bending over her. Their eyes locked as he desperately freed her body from the constraints of the robe. She could think of nothing but the need to feel his body against hers, and her arms gathered him to her. He breathed her name against her hair, repeating it along her cheek until she stopped his murmuring with her mouth. His tongue sought hers with an urgency that seared and scorched. She answered his demand by arching her back and thrusting her hips upward, and then, ever so slowly, she opened her legs so that his hand could slide immediately to the inside of her thigh. The skin there was silky soft, hot and moist.

His mouth began to trace a delicious pattern of pleasure along her throat, across the swell of her breast to capture its throbbing nipple. She could barely moan, "Yes ... darling ..." His head was a blur in the darkness but her fingers easily and eagerly found the thickness of his hair. He raised his face to seek her mouth once more and a ragged gasp escaped his lips. She pressed her palms flat against his chest and began to fumble with the buttons on his shirt. "Help me take your clothes off," she breathed.

Now their bodies came together in complete abandon. She revelled in the feel of the hair on his chest against her nipples as her hands moved over his hot flesh. With little urging she lifted her knees and embraced him totally. He was deep inside her now, and each thrust brought a new wave of rapture such as she had never known before. Finally she knew the truth. Only love could incite such pleasure. Just when she thought that neither of them could take much more, he took her to the very brink of endurance and, incredibly, together, they spiralled into a final and total ecstasy ...

— From *Dream Feast*

The sexiest romance

Try to imagine the sexiest romance you can. Maybe it would be tempestuous, maybe dreamy. Maybe there are intense ups and downs, or maybe it continues to build, day by day, to that "final and total ecstasy". You can fill this dream with all kinds of details: wooing, excitement, confusion, desire, doubts, wild passion, fear and resistance, touching, letting go, resolution, winning, anger, jealousy, and of course — pretty much part of every great romance — great sex.

It turns out that this romance you come up with will be the blueprint for this book. Is that because we presume to know everything about you? Not at all. Actually, just the opposite. We do presume, but our presumption is that *you* know everything about you. You are naturally going to fill in the blanks for you. You are the person who is going to author your relationships, and whatever your needs are in love and sex are the needs which will drive that relationship and drive that romance.

But we should stop a moment. Aren't relationship and romance different things? Isn't romance just a kind of fairy tale, like above, whereas "relationship" is real, mature, sensible and responsible? And not as much fun, unfortunately. Your authors may have what is today a rather rare point of view about man-woman relationships. We are convinced that sex and romance are the valid measures of a successful relationship. Your relationship is unlike anything else. It isn't just about being "old friends", for instance, or about being "used to each other". It certainly isn't a case of role-playing. Nor is it an "even trade": your relationship is not a business partnership.

Instead, when you are experiencing the heights, the full pleasure, of your relationship, there is only one way to describe it — vital, vibrant romance. And this is the romance you have just imagined for yourself. This book will therefore be about *your* relationships, not ours. At no time will you need to change your wants to suit us or anyone else. In fact, just the opposite is going to happen: in reading this book, you will be going in an entirely new direction, delving ever more deeper into exactly what you do want. And when you find that out, you are going to start getting it.

But this subject of sex bothers some people, even irritates them. Sex and romance can seem so "simple-minded", after all. There are all kinds of rich and valuable areas in life — why do we have to make such a big deal out of sex? Your authors certainly agree that life is full of a variety of rich and rewarding areas: family and home, religion, career, maybe education, or travel, or fitness. It seems as if our lives are full of many possible "Tv-screens" which can monopolise our attention. Sometimes we turn our channel to "friendship" and turn off "parenting". Or we turn on "work" and turn off "relationship". But you may have noticed that, no matter what other channels are playing at the time, "sex" is the one that is never switched off.

Whether it's fantasies, vague desires, strong attractions, daydreams, night dreams, sexual doubts, even denials of sexual feelings, on some level sex is the channel that is always on. Of course, there is more to relationships between men and women than sex. But we are stating that it would almost be better if there weren't. Sex is part and parcel of our healthy human drive for pleasure, the pleasure that fuels the joy and accomplishment of a turned-on and productive relationship.

So what are we waiting for? Let's have some of it!

The seduction

But let's slow down a bit. Jumping into pleasure with both feet isn't going to get us there. Pursuing pleasure as if it's a goal or destination turns pleasure into a *thing*. Essentially, it makes pleasure very unpleasurable! We may recollect that pleasure has something to do with enjoying the process of getting there. Isn't pleasure all about smelling the roses along the way? It may be that real pleasure is about gradually opening up to the pleasurable opportunities which are already available to us. So instead of going into a harangue about how you are missing out on life's delights, we would simply like to remind you of the feeling of a gradual opening up to pleasure. We would simply like to offer you a bit of seduction.

The seduction is ninety-nine per cent of any great romance: it is the courtship, the foreplay, the give-and-take of attraction and rejection. During a courtship, or during foreplay, your native sensuality is gradually and naturally increased. You find yourself being slowly swept off your feet and encircled until more and more of you becomes involved. If you like oranges, you are brought oranges. If you like chocolate, you are brought chocolate. If you like red and white roses, you are brought deep reds and creamy whites. Or if you are out of touch with your body right now — the insides of your arms, your skin, the back of your neck — these areas are slowly touched, encircled, involved.

So you can see why we ask you to fill in the blanks. Do you in fact *like* red and white roses? You have to find out what is a seduction for you before you can be seduced. It may seem contradictory, but in this way you can start to be responsible for your own seduction. You can begin to master the seductive paradox of being "swept off your feet in control". So in this book, we intend to involve all of you. Every part of you. Your thoughts, your loves, your frustrations, your confusions, your needs, your demands, your doubts, your fantasies.

The first part of our little courtship, however, will be unique. Right off the top, we need to deal with something … distasteful. Imagine that you are actually making love. Passionate love. Let's say you are feeling completely adored and nurtured when you notice pieces of plaster coming off your wall and falling in your face. Or let's say you look out from your bed, and there, smack in the middle of the bedroom, is an ugly, greasy, ratty, motel-orange sofa. You also see that on top of it is a pile of old work papers sliding off. If this is the condition of your bedroom, then you are not taking care of yourself. And you are not being taken care of.

We need to clean up. Cleaning house is probably not the dream-date of a lifetime, but you should know that it is an act of love and caring for yourself. It is also the first step in you gaining power over your world. The particular house we are interested in happens to be your mind. Some of us may live in quite tasteful surroundings in real life, but we walk around with filthy shacks for our mental housing.

No more homework

So what is the first thing to hit the garbage can? *Work*. It's that stack of papers sliding to the floor. The moment you work hard on your relationship is the moment you are selling pleasure down the river. Remember the dating workshop Maureen spoke of? Her girlfriend had three hours of homework to do each weekend for five weeks. What utter displeasure. We all seem to be working very hard at exactly what it's *not* all about. For this reason, your authors shy away from most "how-to" work books and seminars. The how-to approach can be fine — often it is helpful, even courageous — but it is rarely fun. When pleasure becomes another goal, no pleasure can actually be experienced. Honest human pleasure is just too foreign from that kind of goal-driven work strategy.

If we were writing about overhauling an engine, we could say, "Great — this is *how-to*." Or baking a cake — no problem. You can bake a cake even if your day has been lousy. But be a fiery seductress? That's tougher. This time around, you are involved in it head-to-toe. Try to tell a woman who has been devastated by men that she should learn to trust more. Or try to tell a woman who hasn't allowed herself to show anger for 20 years to plan romantic walks in the moonlight. God, she wants to, you know it. But it isn't going to happen. Even if you are initially successful with the how-to approach, you can easily get burned out and revert to old ways again. The how-to approach is just too much work. And working at pleasure is a horror. It's a contradiction; and it's a sacrilege.

So we're not going to tell you to change yourself. We hope that is a relief. Yet for many, this may be a disappointment, because they are addicted to *working on themselves*. But pleasure is different. Do you remember the experience of love and of romance? Isn't that when you found out that there is someone who adores every part of you just the way you are? That you don't have to change one little thing? And although that may be a bit hard to accept at first, before long you find yourself basking in the adoration. In the same way, we refuse to give you more ways to beat yourself up for not being super-woman. We refuse to prescribe for any illnesses here. We're only going to *de*scribe your health. Before long, you'll find yourself basking in the native pleasure that is yours to enjoy.

Of course, you may be all fired up about fixing your relationships, or making your relationships better. But understand that if you're still convinced something is not quite okay with you, we guarantee that you will end up in a no-fun, burned-out muddle. You'll wonder what went wrong. You'll wonder vaguely why you're a failure. You'll wonder why men are such jerks. And you'll wonder, "If relationships are such a natural part of human life, why are they such a pain?"

Your strange bedfellow

There is a simple answer. In your bedroom, right under those papers we just threw out, is that ratty, grubby, motel-orange sofa. It has been crowding your life for as long as you can remember. You sit on it, lie on it, make detours around it, soil your clothes on it. Often you make love on it. You have become so accustomed to it, you may not know it's there. This particular sofa is like an attitude. It's the way society views pleasure. It's absolutely the strangest bedfellow you can imagine.

We use the word *society* to mean those common influences that can affect a nation's people. In many nations, for example, an influence is patriarchy, a general support of male authority. In other countries, individualism may tend to colour the thinking of its citizens. In the same way, there is something so fundamental to our society that you may not have realised it. Put simply, society is not big on seeking pleasure. The society you grew up in is big on financial security, material progress and avoiding being dominated by others — and these are certainly good things. But for the most part, your society considers pleasure to be hedonistic, decadent and irresponsible. Even low-class, embarrassing or dirty.

On the other hand, we've been raised to believe that "suffering" somehow builds character — *noble* suffering. At a party, there is usually someone who spares us no detail talking about the horrors of their operation, but they would never consider mentioning the incredible orgasm they had the night before. Setting out to pursue pleasure is not acceptable for most of us. It only seems right in a kind of abstract way; maybe

10

if it's in the next life. And of course, we also have to *deserve* such pleasure ... which shoots us right back into noble suffering in the here and now.

No pleasure, no pleasure

"No pain, no gain" might be the latest version of our noble suffering. But our motto in this book is "No pleasure, no pleasure." No pleasure is its own punishment. If you are trying to make your relationship better with your man, and deep within you is the idea that work, pain and suffering are necessary things, you will discover work, pain and suffering in your relationship. If you think that the devil lives in the pleasures of life, you will find him. Just don't be surprised that in your day-to-day living, pleasure almost always takes a back seat.

When was the last time your man filled your bedroom with flowers? When was the last time he swept you off your feet? Or spent half a day in bed with you? When last did your man's face light up to see you? When was the last time you felt really attractive to him? Or felt adored by him? Or just had fun with him? When was the last time your body, your skin, felt good and alive with his touch? Aren't these good things? How could you ever be convinced that something is wrong with such joy and pleasure?

Touch me

Just the opposite is true. Pleasure is basic to life. Aren't we naturally built to enjoy pleasure? Isn't it what we naturally pursue? Even amoebas move instinctively toward food and pull away from electric shock. Of course, we can always engage in lofty discussions about which pleasures should be labelled "lower" pleasures and which "higher". But be clear — such discussions are still *all about pleasure*. In addition, there are potent arguments that both the "higher" and the "lower" pleasures are utterly, and equally, necessary.

For instance, human infants who are deprived of the "lower" pleasure of physical touch fail to develop normally, either physically or mentally. Untouched children in institutions are physically stiff and emotionally wooden. They are unusually quiet and underweight; they sleep excessively. But when these same children are touched regularly, they start to revive. They even gain weight. Diseases of the skin are sometimes healed by this pleasurable touch. Hospital patients who are touched by their attendants have recuperated up to three times faster than those who are not. There are also reports of autistic children, and some schizophrenics, who have been speeded toward recovery by being regularly massaged, touched, held.

Your skin is the largest organ of your body, touch the mother of your senses. Touch is the very first sense you ever developed, the earliest experience you had of your own identity, and is your most fundamental communication with the world. Touch was also your first link of love, security and pleasure with another human being, your mother. Because touch is such a fundamental source of pleasure, some cultures refine and elaborate touching into amazing arrays of sensual patterns which arouse, prolong and evoke intense pleasure and communication between the sexes.

But in our society, touching is highly suspicious. Even that most crucial touching of an infant by its own mother has come under some outrageous attacks over the years. At the turn of the century, it took form as a "modern", scientific war against the pleasurable rocking of infants in arms and cradles. In mid-century, it took form as a modern, scientific war against breast feeding. And today, we are still modern and scientific when we separate newborns from their mothers' touch by sweeping them off to hospital nurseries. Sometimes we continue to be modern and scientific by making sure our children are kept in remote cribs, separated from us until we hear a cry for food.

So why this hostility to touch? The answer is simple. Touching is pleasurable. That touching which allows infants to develop normally, which allows patients to heal, and which, by imparting love and security, allows children to grow physically and mentally is not something that is painful for these subjects. It is pleasurable.

Touching is always dangerously close to being sexual, of

course. We generally allow for a little bit of cautious, social touching, but not much. If we enjoy a social hug too much, we generally believe that something is wrong. But what we are calling "social" touching — that is, "non-sexual" touching — may simply be *less* sexual touching. The real difference between your elbow and your clitoris is forty-five sensory receptors per square inch versus 900. There is simply, physically, more touch down there.

It is notable that research shows women's sexual response to be more centred around physical touch than men's sexuality, which is more visual. This happens to coincide pretty well with our society today. If the pleasure of touch is important to women, but women are mostly excluded from positions of power, guess what also gets excluded? A society which diminishes the status of women would also be a society which diminishes the importance of touch and the physical pleasure related to it.

A *scientific pain*

One of the very latest assaults on human pleasure is again a scientific one. If we consider the many reports that have come out in recent years, romance, pleasure and love are being reduced to the survival of the species and a few nifty brain chemicals.

Now science, *as science*, is wonderful. All the experimental details in these reports are certainly accurate — the research, the measurements, the chemistry. But the implicit point of view emerging here is that the chemicals *are* the experience. Certainly, as any coffee drinker knows, imbibe the chemical and an experience follows. But science cannot come close to explaining what experience is in the first place. What is the witnessing of that chemical change? Therefore, in general terms, it would probably be unwise to look to science for the tribute that human experience demands. Nonetheless, some researchers wish to put the most profound of our experiences — love — into the same dead world of jostled molecules and stupid evolution.

Are we all just machines multiplying numbly into the future? If you feel that you are doing yourself a favour by viewing your life, love and ecstasy as cogs in the Big Machine, then have a ball. But you will notice that at that very same instant, your power goes away. No longer are you actively engaged in this life; rather, you are a cog, a drone. Human pleasure is not a cog in the machine. It is instead the profoundly meaningful call of our very essence.

This world of ours is starved for a revival of pleasure. Typically, after we experience a couple of years of love and caresses in our lives, the closest we seem to come to pleasure today is in the *avoidance of pain.* This way, we keep our focus on pain. Nobody can accuse us of being greedy, shallow or self-indulgent, because, after all, we are just fixing the pain. In this regard, our society has triumphed. Nearly every other Tv commercial wants to sell us pain-relievers. Or "social embar-rassment"-relievers. Our attention is always focused on the pain. The pain of violence is a guaranteed box-office draw. The pain of other people is the daily bread of our newspapers.

In addition, a natural consequence of such pain is "negativity". Some have estimated that each of us receive about 37,000 criticisms from our parents before we are barely seven years old. It isn't our parents' fault, of course: they probably heard 370,000 criticisms from their folks. It's just that we may be so steeped in pain and negativity that we cannot even see it.

Because now, the criticisms seem to be going the other way. Instead of saying what we want, we criticise what we dislike. Instead of going for what is good in life, we get stuck trying to fix the bad. This orientation to the negative is right there in our relationships. Right there in our bedrooms. It's smelly, ratty and motel-orange — we're sitting on it. We are permeated with the negativity of a pain-oriented society.

Supreme laws of the universe

So everyone should be positive all of a sudden, right? No. That's just more work. You don't need to start walking around grinning and positive. There are people who are convinced that acting this way makes them better people, more civilised people, more moral people. But happiness and pleasure aren't going to descend out of the sky and into your life by pretending. Nor, by the way, are we telling you to think positively so that you can land the job, or get the man, or win the lottery. All of these artificial behaviours do nothing but turn your pleasure into an unnatural chore.

In our little programme, you can be whatever way you want to be. Along with this, however, we do have useful information for you — "fixing the bad" is a total fiction. It never happens. If you have ever tried to work out the hurt and anger in your relationships, or worry yourself into a feeling of security, you will understand what we mean. We all keep thinking that enough pain will somehow bring forth pleasure. In fact, *pain only brings more pain.* Luckily, however, going for the good brings more good — *pleasure brings more and more pleasure.* These are laws of the universe.

It's not difficult to see that pain is about pursuing the negative and destructive, and pleasure is about pursuing the positive and productive. That is, what you *don't want* has always been about your pain. What you *do want* is all about your pleasure. So if you are interested at all in pursuing the pleasurable, you should know that at some point it involves looking a bit to the positive.

Should you read this book?

Of course, being positive usually seems acceptable, but this discussion about pleasure is where people get uncomfortable. Consciously seek out pleasure? Where could that lead? Won't that mark the end of civilisation? We're all supposed to become hedonists? We're all supposed to become ". . . decadent and irresponsible? Even low-class, or embarrassing, or dirty?" We're sure you get the point. Society's ideas have crawled inside our own heads, our own bedrooms.

Nonetheless, the first thing you need to find out is whether you should even be reading this book. We know this is a peculiar thing to bring up, but it's decision time. We are cleaning house, but you may not realise how attached you are to that painful old sofa. If you feel your life should be a penance of some sort, or that suffering is a good thing to have, this book is not for you. You may say (along with many) that you want fun and romance, but actually getting them may turn out to be too strange, too foreign, a whole different set of habits, responses and ways of thinking about things. You need to find out quickly. If you feel that pleasure is morally wrong, selfish, unintelligent, silly, irresponsible or a waste of time, then you will get very little from this book.

On the other hand, you have made it this far in reading this book. Dangerous subject! Have you hidden the book so your man won't see it? Many of us have the assumption that if we are able to receive more pleasure, someone must lose. If you get what you want, your man cannot. Besides, everyone might think you are selfish and shallow if you show too much interest in being pleasured. But if you have chosen to investigate this book, you have dipped your little toe into a quest for pleasure *despite* society. Your authors would like to invite you to continue on in. The water really is fine.

It may be that some of this journey to pleasure is new, but don't confuse that with struggle and pain. It is neither. If you still have doubts, you might consider the experience of being in love. We wonder if penance and suffering is better than this. Are your obstacles and frustrations better than this? Is your love a "waste of time"? Your authors feel that your love may be the only thing that is not a waste of time.

Maureen: *The journey to pleasure*

I have to tell you, it takes guts to go for pleasure. It takes guts to put the joy of life foremost. There are so many addictions which are not pleasurable. Being angry at the world, at wars, at religion, politics, parents, teachers and men. Or being motivated by guilt or stress. Sometimes this journey to pleasure could sound scary, but nothing will be more worthwhile.

If pleasure sounds interesting, stay tuned. If you can handle steak and lobster served to you on a golden plate, then, sister,

16

you've arrived. This book is for those women who want to thrive, because once we find the good, we'll be going for more. More and more pleasure. Fun, freedom, romance, progress and energy — these are the prizes.

Chapter 3

The Different Minority

*Where you begin to sort out the influences of male
society on your life*

We may be making some headway moving that repulsive sofa,
the love of pain, out of the door. So are we just about finished?
Not quite. We can't make love in a pigsty, and neither can you.
We're telling you that you're better than that. We're here to tell
you that it is a labour of love to continue to clean house. Keep
in mind where we're going. Keep in mind the pleasure.

So have you noticed that in really great romances, usually
the woman first becomes infuriated by the man involved? As
viewers, we are usually entertained by this, because we know
this marks the beginning of intense chemistry and "juice"
between the two. So our small courtship will also try to include
your anger, but in a different way. Unfortunately, we are taking
the romance away for a moment. We're leaving only the anger.
We must take a good look at the way women are treated in our
society. It is like plaster that keeps falling in your face.

Are you second class?

In South Africa, blacks outnumber whites ten to one. Yet under
apartheid, they were still a "minority" because they didn't have
any mines, factories or land — in other words, wealth and
power. Women in many countries outnumber men slightly, but
because they have limited access to power, they are also a
minority. Whether you know it or not, like it or not, want to
think about it or not, society is again creeping into your bedroom.
First, society typically views human pleasure as sinful or silly.
Second, it casts you, a woman, as a second-class citizen.

18

Maureen: *Presumptuous me*

For a while, I thought times were changing. But I keep running into incredible aggravation on this most basic topic. I recently did a presentation for training the staff of an upmarket restaurant. As usual, I felt fairly confident and professional reviewing my background and giving the owner an analysis of his training needs based on the research I had performed for him. However, at some point during this conversation I started to feel peculiar. I couldn't put my finger on it at first, but then it became obvious. He was angry at me and attacked my credentials and expertise. What had I done to elicit this? He finally said that I, a woman, had no right to tell him what would be best for his business.

Some people still think second-class status for women is completely natural. Men are physically stronger, so they should be higher on the social heap and so on. But this is pretty silly. In one well researched book, *The Chalice and the Blade*, Riane Tennen Eisler describes complex, flourishing societies in ancient times that seem to have been based on men and women acting in equal partnerships in work and commerce. Apparently not all cultures have felt they must pit men's and women's needs against each other.

Of course, some proclaim how the new "information age" will establish wonderful political and workplace equality. And, yes, it does seem to take much of the pressure off strict sex roles. But high-tech isn't going to light up your relationships. Passion in a printout? Turn-on in a time sheet? Swept off your feet and stuck on the sales phone? Yuk. Satellite conference calls may be neat, but your own psychological "conference calls" are still being carried on with Cinderella and Doris Day. You really don't have a chance to explore your own personal beauty and humanity. All that's left is to model your parents' behaviours, seek out a few responses you can call your own, and privately compare them with the cultural folklore. In this arena, of course, feminism has had an important impact.

What do you think about feminism?

Pam: Overrated: women have always innately known that they have the power to manipulate. I think that a lot of women's liberation groups are still manipulating by using reverse psychology for the purpose of controlling men.

Andrea: Totally necessary and empowering. It just has to happen in order for everyone to realise their potentials as human beings.

Kathleen: It's needed, but it sounds like some feminists want you to hate men.

Candy: Sometimes I think it's really lame. It makes women look silly when they go overboard.

Sandra: I've written feminist papers. I've even led feminist women's groups. It's been good, yet I'm ready for some new information as well. I'm interested in additional perspectives.

Marjorie: I think it's time, but some women go too far and think they are better than men.

Anne: I feel that feminist issues have given me an important leg to stand on in the workplace. I've been able to receive a lot more respect now from my male co-workers.

Ours is not a feminist book. Other books do feminism better than we do. We like some feminism; we question other feminism. But many women think feminism is the "F" word. This isn't just because of their resistance to changing sex roles. There is another reason for some women's rejection of feminism, and we touch on it later. For now, however, whether you love it or hate it, there are a few facts mentioned under "feminism" that we must take a look at. They are not very shocking. They are more like announcing that the earth is round.

Though it varies from nation to nation, western industrial countries offer working women overall only three-quarters the pay that men make. In most cases, the very same work gets paid a lower wage if a woman performs it. When both sexes are employed in the same occupations, women are often given different titles than men to justify their lower wages. This, despite the fact that women turn out to take fewer breaks from their jobs, as well as to work harder overall (112 per cent that of men).

Even women with similar education make less money than their male counterparts. This holds true in both third-world and industrialised countries. Women are also regularly excluded from male power networks in business. Even with recent, publicised gains, women are still under-represented politically and remain unequal before the law in many countries.

The game

There are enough studies about these issues to show that the point is made. Just on the level of the facts, ma'am, women fare poorly in the workplace, politics and other traditionally male spheres. Of course, this barely scratches the surface. Women in less industrial nations usually fall somewhere between humiliated and enslaved.

We've all heard such information, of course. But by itself, this material is like the football before a game starts: nobody really cares where (or what) it is. Where everyone goes crazy is in the *game,* the argument. Who has the ball now? Religion? Is it women's spiritual duty to remain second-class citizens? Or is it women's genetic differences, their "child-bearing natures", that psychologically limit their access to power? Politics? Is it commanding domination by men, old-boy hierarchies and male brainwashing in religion, culture and ethics that keeps women down? Now, you see, we can have an exciting controversy and become very angry.

But oddly enough, this time, we're not going to take the bait. Why not? Because none of these points of view is going to help you. Our book operates only *within your relationship.* Within your relationship, the view that genetics holds women down serves little purpose other than to blame and belittle you. And within your relationship, the view that society holds women down serves little purpose other than to blame and belittle your man.

We assume you are tired of blaming and belittling in your relationship. This book is about pleasure — and blame is poison to pleasure. So we're not going to hide our political heads in the sand; we're just going to stay out of the blaming. We're going to narrow our focus to simply the way it is. The way it is right now — justified or unjustified, right or wrong, fair or unfair — is that rocks are hard, water is wet, and women are a minority.

Rude awakenings

Yet if blaming poisons our pleasure, why invite the temptation by bringing in politics? Doesn't politics just confound the issue? Yes, it does. Unfortunately, however, it confounded the issue long before this book was written. The status of women translates into your everyday life whether you are aware of it or not. Even if you don't know a thing about work-world statistics, or you are unable to "prove" your minority status (or are totally uninterested in doing so) you still feel it. You don't think about it. You live inside it.

We have to realise that women get it from the first day of their lives: "It's a girl!" versus "IT'S A BOY!!!" It doesn't have to be a threat of rape or violence. From sexual jokes to sexual harassment, there is a horde of digs and diminishments that are an integral part of women's lives. So what is the response of "living inside" such second-class status? About what could be expected from any being with an IQ higher than cheese. It makes women angry.

Maureen: *Anger as a child*

The first recollection I have of my own anger is when I was five years old. I deeply resented the bossiness of my eight-year-old brother. Because he had to take care of me, I was a burden on him, and he took it out on me with a domineering attitude, forcing me to obey his commands. He was no doubt impatient with my girlish whims, and the fact that I had trouble keeping pace with him and his friends just made it worse. But being too small to fight, I was often left feeling frustrated and humiliated.

This story would be just about sibling rivalry if it weren't for how I remember my parents acting one day when I was left in my brother's charge. This time it was more than I could bear. Rebellion arose within me from my deepest roots — I wouldn't let him strip me of my dignity. I didn't have those words, but I had the anger. The next time he yelled at me, I walked into the middle of the road and lay down, telling him I would rather die than be ordered around. He ran after me, grabbed my arm and twisted it as he dragged me off the road.

For hours I was in excruciating pain with a distorted arm twisted up my back. My parents finally arrived and took me to the hospital. But even though I was in such obvious pain, they refused to hear my side of the story. Instead, they immediately sympathised with my brother, and became angry with me. To them, my point of view was completely invalid. He was the boy, you see, but I was just a girl. From here on out, I quickly learned that men had the upper hand. I was not an equal, and my resentment grew.

The biggest taboo

What are little girls made of, anyway? Sugar and spice and everything nice. If you are nice, you've won half the battle of being a successful woman. If you are "not very nice", it is spelled b - i - t - c - h.

"No matter what, do not be a bitch," is the creed of nearly all women. A good woman would never show her anger ... only a bitch would do that. But society still has this interesting "cover story" about women — that little girls are everything nice. Lurking underneath it, however, could well be *bad bad Betty BadBitch*. Even though you experience a lot of aggravation just by being a woman in this society, you must generally remain nice. Acting like a bitch is the biggest taboo. In the work environment, the "aggressive" woman — whether successful or not — is usually disliked by both sexes. It's the exact opposite for men, of course. We all know that "nice guys finish last". At the same time, we can't attribute all of this attitude to some vague society out there, for some of it comes from other sources.

You may be a bit of a co-conspirator in this nice-girl thing. That doesn't mean you should be ashamed of it: humans probably all want to be nice, finally. The pleasurable experience of loving, for instance, is extremely generous and nurturing and nice. Almost everyone has had a little nurturing at least once in their life, and it was *nice*. Yet women seem to find themselves more in the thick of this than men. It goes with the territory. Women can become mothers, and mothers often find themselves monitoring rather intimate and sensitive relationships among mates and children. Even if you're not a mother, you're possibly in a relationship. Your man may respond positively to binding emotions like warmth, tenderness and kindness. Whether in a relationship, family or both, how can anyone really slight you for being kind and nurturing? So the first thing you should know is that *you are not selling out your sex by being warm or supportive or loving in your relationships*. And no serious feminist would claim you are.

But here's the rub. Anger seems to crop up in everyone's life from time to time, but for women there is no place to express this anger. For the sake of your relationship, you haven't had the option to express even normal anger. On the other hand, it would be oafish of us to tell you to start dumping anger everywhere. Instead, we're just at the stage of acknowledging anger, and acknowledging that you're not some kind of evil person for having it. What to do about anger comes later.

Tantrum politics

Of course, there are excellent reasons for you to hold back your anger. These include feeling you will lose your man, or that any anger you let out will snowball until you are completely out of control. A specific fear many women have is that others will find out that under their nice personality is an ugly and destructive one. So for most women, anger is a poignant issue. Yet it isn't one for men, because they're allowed, even encouraged, to express it.

Which adds to the problem. Let's face it — you happen to

24

be intimate with a larger, more physically powerful human who feels just fine expressing himself. That's enough to check anyone's personal fury. Want to know what an angry *man* does when a bigger man comes into the room? He gets very nice, very quickly. Same thing as you. It's what we refer to as "being smart".

James: *Surprise at home base*

My wife and I recently had a conversation — well, argument — that was an eye-opener for me. I was showing her a video I had produced to get her thoughts about it. Halfway through, she commented candidly on something that needed work. At this point, I swore because I knew she was right but was tired of working on the project. At the end, however, she said only, "It hangs together very well." She made no other mention of the part that needed work.

I looked at her. "Except for the part in the middle, right?"

"Yeah, well — it wasn't bad," she answered.

I sat there for a moment, puzzled: she was now being nice. I felt I had already accepted that I had to go back and fix that portion and had geared up mentally for the job. But now somehow I felt I had no more support, because it "wasn't bad". I said, "I don't feel like I'm getting the truth. Before, you said that portion didn't work at all."

"I know — I already said that."

"But then you said it wasn't that bad," I replied.

"No, it isn't horrible," she said.

So taxiing my plane onto the runway of an argument, I said, "So which is it — bad or not?"

She explained that she noticed it, but I didn't have to get so upset about it.

"I wasn't upset at you," I said. "I was just upset because I knew I had to change it." I added, "You don't have to pretend you didn't say it."

"I'm not pretending," she shot back.

"I'm just getting mixed signals," I said.

25

Our little tiff bumped along until she granted me that her milder remarks were based on instinctive fear. She said she felt as though she were walking on eggshells. She was right — I *was* upset about the extra work. But I now also understand that I had sat there in my very tall, 198 cm body spouting that anger. Any human smaller than I (there are a few) would probably do whatever they needed to escape that reaction, even retract something said.

Yet something was still off. I remember saying, possibly a bit densely, "But you knew that I wasn't angry at *you* — why would you be afraid when there was no real threat to you?"

She thought for a moment: "It wasn't exactly fear of you. It was fear that I would set you off."

I asked her, "So what kind of person do you think I am who can't handle the truth when I ask for it?"

She blurted, "You're weak."

Honesty usually renders me speechless. I managed to stay cool: "Okay, you think I'm weak."

She added helpfully, "Weak and insecure."

This one also slipped in without reaction, but I was aware of a kind of icy emotional grip crawling over me. I gulped. "Okay … Gotcha. Weak and insecure."

"I have to make sure exactly how I talk about your work, or you'll get upset."

But it seemed there was something else she wanted to say. So I pushed ever farther into self-ruin and said, "So what is that to you? What do you believe about that?" No response. "Does it make you feel happy or sad or what?" She was shaking her head, frowning earnestly. And then in a burst — "It makes me angry. I am really angry about it."

When she looked up, however, she was grinning. Then grinning widely. She laughed. (We apparently got to the bottom of it.) At this point, I felt the need to step in and clearly state that I am not weak and not insecure and not blah-blah, but she wasn't paying much attention. "I know you're not," she said, laughing again. "You're just a man. You're the same as the men at work. I always have to make it easy for their childish feelings."

The very book I was working on seemed to be leaping off the computer screen in realistic Sensurround. My loving companion thought I was a jerk because I was a man. At this point, she went on to give me examples of the men at her workplace. Then she said, "Men have the control, yet they're incredibly stupid. They're insensitive with others and always have to be so damn right. Then to top it off, they're the ones who end up being liked all the time.

"They always get the credit, even when they think of things using my ideas as springboards. But because they grab onto it and communicate with a lot of excitement, they get the credit. I'm just sick of having to make it all okay for them. I play the game, I act nice, but I won't give them the strokes they want. Why don't they go and do all their primping and strutting on someone else's time?" She added, "It's also frustrating, because these are the same men I go to in order to feel acknowledged. These are the same people I always try to get approval from."

Such frustration is standard fare. Second class means that first class holds the emotional cards. First class sets the standards. So, for having the least opportunity to express anger, women seem to have the most to express it about. At least other kinds of minorities are able to express their anger from time to time. A minority group usually gets segregated in some way: townships (South Africa), or ghettos, or reservations, or even "servants' quarters". Of course, segregation is no thrill — the freedom to express a little anger can't redress the misery and inequality of being segregated.

But the difference with *the different minority* is that you are literally sleeping with the enemy. This whole second-class thing enters into the fragile nucleus of relationships, child-rearing and family. These traditionally "feminine" social domains are fraught with these most feminine of issues. This is the domain we treat in this book. It is a bewildering mixture of love, frustration, support, nurturing, possession, resistance, power and dependence.

Maureen: *Whose money are we using?*

An important issue for many women — one that came up in my marriage — is money and dependence. The fact that most of my money came through my husband's business always made me feel unequal in that relationship. But my guilt was undeserved. I worked alongside my husband seven days a week, took care of three children, cleaned house, cooked, shopped, went to PTA meetings and school events, organised family vacations and performed home repairs. But for 18 hours a day nonstop, I walked around with the feeling that I was the lesser contributor. When eventually we broke up, I remember that Bill wanted 60 per cent of our assets against my 40 per cent. His own lawyer disagreed with him, but my meek and guilty conscience had me thinking maybe Bill was right.

Finally, my wealthy aunt sat me down and straightened me out. She said that in addition to the other work I was performing, I contributed the energy and the power to the relationship. "I see your family and I feel it," she said. This was new information for me at the time, but after a while I began to understand. I was the energy of love, support, appreciation, fun, sensuality and sexuality that fuelled all our productivity and income. In fact, I was incredibly angry at myself for years after my divorce for how meekly I acted in that marriage. It was ridiculous.

As we discuss later, self-esteem is absolutely essential to your being a self-possessed and powerful member of your man/woman partnership. Until then, just know that it is important to understand our society and its views about women. Take how we are trained to view women's bodies. For one example, society is quite silly in how it views women's genitalia. Girls receive instructions something like this: "Don't play with it, don't touch it, don't look at it, don't talk about it. It's nasty, it's smelly, it's dirty ... save it for someone you love."

Nice girls

Then there are things like men's reactions to menstruation. Such fear notwithstanding, menstruation itself can be an ordeal. In fact, for about a third of all women, menstruation seems to occur in a physical state somewhere between flu and coma. As one woman put it, "Every month, I pray to be delivered from these symptoms, and every month I end up shouting, 'Screw you, too!'" Hmm … not very nice.

Which is the point. From all the physical and social craziness of being female, women are regularly struggling to be nice. As a result, there are many nice women around. We know that you, for instance, are probably a nice woman. And a good mate. And a good mother. A good person and a nice person. And "nice" is fine, remember. Nurturing is nice; love is nice; support is nice. Nice is a good thing. Nobody is telling you to grab your man and dump out all your anger. That would be a shabby way to carry on.

Social issues and relationship issues seem to be a rotten mix. Want to stand up angrily for your rights when you are dating someone? He will go away. How about in marriage? He may also go away. Anger creates divisiveness in families, even if the men don't leave. Anger and blame and political polarisation don't seem to work in relationships. They are bulls in china shops. And more than anything else, this may be the reason many women dislike the straight feminist line. Feminism seems to attack the things they hold dear.

For instance, feminism would probably encourage you to take your anger and make it political. That only makes sense. If the source of your anger is political, then use that anger to change the political world. But the problem is that anger is like tar — it tends to stick to you, to weaken you. If you can make an opponent angry, for instance, you've won half the battle. You've taken away his or her control, stability and ability to be effective.

This is the crux of the matter. Whether you are able to trace unfair treatment back to politics or just to the fact that your man is *such a jerk sometimes*, you are still the one who is stuck with this issue. On one hand, it seems that your anger is perfectly justified. On the other hand, harbouring this justified anger eventually tears up any of the pleasure in your relationship. We cannot make this choice for you between harbouring anger, or avoiding it. But it is important to know that anger destroys.

Maureen: *Anger and choice*

I certainly could have wrapped my anger up in politics: it's easy to see that men and women are unequal on this planet. I remember my father telling my mother what she should and shouldn't do and rarely treating her with much respect or decency. But though my parents were as much a part of the "politics of gender" as anyone else, my own experience of them is still personal. My anger is personal, so my growth beyond it has to be personal.

The anger I experienced in childhood stayed with me for about 35 years. Though I was oblivious to it, anger still formed the background of all my relationships with men. It was a constant barrier to any pleasure in my relationships and in life itself.

So I could have done very different things with my anger. A woman I know, Annie, takes her anger out on men by keeping her complete independence at all costs. She seems to attract men easily, but then enjoys watching her prey fall slowly and hopelessly in love. It's a classic case of "spider to the fly". Once her man falls in love with her, she starts flirting around with new prey. The current victim gets driven to distraction, feeling jealous, outraged and obsessed. He then does something crazy and out of control — sometimes violent. Her relationships end in disaster, a scenario that has been Annie's for 43 years. Her motto is, "No man will ever tell me what to do; no man will ever own me."

She may be right. Yet as long as her hurt and anger remain wrapped up in this word, "independence", she can never experience any real pleasure. As long as my anger is wrapped up in the word "politics", I also cannot have any pleasure. Social and political change is essential, but anger just destroys. So I could have taken my anger out on men. Or I could have made it political. But if I did either one, it would still be with me.

In search of middle ground

Don't be mistaken — feminism has been extremely valuable. "Feminist" ideas have challenged many crazy, fairy-tale notions about women, from "the evil temptress" to Cinderella. For instance, it has challenged that modern-day fairy tale, "suburban homemaker". The stay-at-home suburban housewife is a very powerful social image that even today can seem alive and well. New ideas about women are facing it down, but they haven't eliminated it.

It is comical that many people secretly compare their relationships with this idealised and sanitised image of womanhood, although hardly anybody has personal circumstances that could allow it. But that fact doesn't stop two-thirds of us from feeling like failures because we are still comparing ourselves with childhood images of nuclear-family perfection. The reason that perfect ideals like this are rarely seen is simply that they don't work. It's another "rocks are hard, water's wet" issue.

Of course, the complete opposite, a total disintegration of the family, isn't much of an answer either. So people today are busy seeking some sort of middle ground, but it is scarce real estate. The problem with the feminist line is that it has booted, or deadened, male-female sexuality itself. Many women are now trying to find loopholes in the equation, "sexual equals sexist".

Until they do, women continue to live in a world with some very weird options. Some women resolve this problem by embracing one lifestyle extreme or the other: sensuous woman or career killer. Others try to find a compromise, but it is a compromise usually laden with struggles and doubts.

Feminism has shown us that the emperor has no clothes, and that women are second-class citizens. Yet it has also given us an incomplete road map for man-woman relationships. Relationships modelled after feminist issues become politicised, and though that may work for a few, it doesn't work for others.

31

So you are still inside the dilemma. When you mix your struggle to be nice, to be a good daughter/girlfriend/wife/mother, with valid social anger, you get a heady brew indeed. That anger isn't going to evaporate. It isn't going to get released, and it isn't going to go away. Instead, it's going to sneak out (more on that later).

Coming to grips

This raises an important issue, however. Are we telling you to ignore issues of social and political inequality? Absolutely not. Nonetheless, we do have doubt that nurturing anger about those issues will help you. Are we, then, dictating that you should embark on some programme to eliminate your anger? Well, you can try it, but we doubt you will be able to purge your anger as if it were a drain clog. For now, just be aware of some perfectly natural anger, and thereby grant yourself a little freedom and choice about it. Because the more you get what you want in life, the more freedom and choice you end up with.

This whole discussion about anger can be upsetting to read about, and even to write about. Just by thinking about your own anger, it can feel as though it could really do some damage. It could kill. But acknowledging it is the first step in clearing it up. No matter how justified it is, anger is like bad plaster. It keeps falling in your face in the middle of the most pleasurable moments, and you keep pretending it's not there. But when you know that anger is part and parcel of being a woman in this particular world, you might be able to breathe easier.

It's a matter of forgiving yourself. There can be a great personal release when anger is simply acknowledged. Each time anger "falls in your face" — and each time you choose pleasure instead of it — you will be healing your mental home. You will be repairing old problems with new plaster.

Of course, very few will automatically be able to pull up pleasure instead of anger. For now, you are going to need a way to "get there from here". A first step is to understand some differences between men and women. But your power as a woman goes far beyond the psychological tricks and tactics some recent authors have suggested. Not psychology, but *biology*. You are going to get what you want with that pure blast of biological power which you alone control and over which you alone will be a master.

Chapter 4

Vive la Différence, Dammit

Where you find out what men's minds are comprised of

But haven't we advanced beyond old sexual roles to reveal that underneath we're all the same human beings? Yes, men and women are, to a great degree, the same human beings. But this numb and hopeful cliché is mere gloss for the fact that men's and women's minds seem to be cut from two separate moulds. Men and women think differently, they communicate differently, they are motivated differently. The reason your man isn't as easy to get along with as your high-school girlfriend is because he *isn't* your high-school girlfriend.

Strangely enough, when push comes to shove, men are really the ones who believe women are just like them. Men are unlikely to consider a way of operating in the world that is outside their own mode of thinking. They're usually dumbfounded to consider that their wife, girlfriend or mother is a different kind of being. Fewer women seem to have a problem with this, but we're stating it for the record: we don't care if it's training, genetics or both, that man over there is a different creature.

Acknowledging the differences between men and women is not some kind of political back-pedalling. We feel that, except in the most condescending ways, *not enough* attention has been paid to the differences between men and women. Missing these differences ends relationships and destroys lives.

So who is that man?

Men and machines

Once upon a time, we were all little blobs of cells multiplying in our mothers' wombs. Once upon a time, we were all pretty much the same. If no hormone changes had ever occurred, in fact, we would all have developed into one sex — female. But for some of us, at about seven weeks, a couple of chemicals — testosterone and *dihydro*testosterone — attacked. Where they attacked, penis and testicles grew. On this excruciatingly primitive level, men will expect attack for the rest of their lives.

There is absolutely nothing complex about men. We know that they walk, they talk, they smile, they dream, they whisper in your ear, they play with the kids. Some of them even show emotions. But we have important information for you, and the sooner you find this out, the sooner you will have a relationship that thrives. This is the basis of understanding everything in this book, the basis of you getting anything at all from your man. Without this, you will grope in the dark forever. Listen closely and engrave this onto your forehead:

Men are binary machines

"Binary" means "two". It is how computers are made. Computers just respond to a "1" or a "0". Like your man. In any situation, he is either 1 or 0. He is either yes or no. He is either on or off. These are the *only* modes that he operates in. Never be misled into thinking that he has any other state of being, any other smooth transition, any other gradual experience. He does not. What exactly is this 1 and 0? *He is either winning or he is losing.*

Men's entire society is winning and losing. Men are "winners" or they are "losers". There are those who are producers and those who are bums. It may be testosterone, it may be conditioning. There is evidence for both. From the time a little boy is separated from dependency on his mother, the games begin. The winning and losing begin. So men are great game players — sports, business, war, even sex ("scoring"!). It's all men's games, men winning and men losing. Winning and losing are as intense and as emotional as love. In fact, love and winning are probably the same thing for men. The woman a man wins with, he loves; the woman a man loses with, he leaves.

The "thrill of victory, the agony of defeat" is the essence of him. We know he looks cool and controlled, but he lives in an emotional world of threat, fear, conquest and danger. If anything threatens, his first response is to win at all costs — go for the kill. This response may be physical or mental. It may be obstinate, punishing, verbal, sarcastic. It may be criminal. But men are natural killers with emotional hair triggers.

We doubt this is any great news for women. Every year, thousands of women are brutalised or emotionally devastated because they tried to fight with a trained killer. You may be right and noble to fight your man — to point out to him precisely why he is a jerk. But anyone who recommends this to women will have blood on their hands. It's not smart to stick your fingers in a gorilla's eyes.

Winning strategies

Robert Pante, renowned speaker and author of *Dressing for Success*, said it well: "Women try to change men, and men don't try to change women — they just get another woman." Of course, you might want your man to improve in certain ways: more productive, more attentive, more sensitive, or nicer. That's fine. If he is winning with you, he will eventually oblige. But such areas are usually where your man is losing with you. When you criticise your man, you drive him away, and you cast yourself as a victim — powerless, needy and angry.

Maureen: *Marguerite's Test*

"I can't believe it!" Marguerite shouted. Her husband, Carl, had just offered to treat me for lunch. I turned to Marguerite. "What? Is something wrong?" She shook her head. "Carl has never paid for anyone's lunch. I don't know why men always want to treat you. I've been watching you this whole time to see what it is that you do, but I can't figure it out." I was really taken aback. Carl was laughing, but also a little embarrassed.

Marguerite is by no means less attractive than I, and she

was in knots trying to figure out what I did that men responded to. I couldn't think of it at first, and neither could Carl. Then I realised what it was. I enjoy making men feel like winners. In fact, for me, they *are* winners. I consider men to be winners just by virtue of them putting their attention on me. So I give them wins and appreciation. I am committed to pleasure. So I look for what's right about them. It's the only thing that works. And it's the only thing that's fun.

How does a man experience winning? One way with which we're probably familiar is performance: winning a prize or competition. So we have sports, or the ladder of success, or war — these are the primary win/lose games for men. But the biggest win for a man is simple production. That's where you come in. A man wins and feels he is winning when he produces for a woman. Of course we know that this is terribly old-fashioned and restrictive and so forth, but it is the way it is. When women doubt themselves, they doubt their attractiveness, *but when men doubt themselves, they doubt their production*. Whether it be sexual performance, career success, or making you happy, men win by producing. There is a sub-category of this production — men win by solving problems. They have evolved a rather restricted "linear", but still very effective, problem-solving brain.

Maureen: *Plugging him in*

I walked into a store the other day with a broken tape recorder. The counter attendant was a woman, who quickly began to write the item up for repair. But I thought the problem was minor, so I mentioned this to her just as a male assistant was passing by. It was as though I had plugged him in. He stopped in his tracks, took the tape recorder, opened it up and proceeded to check it out with incredible dedication and diligence. After five minutes, however, it was obvious the item needed to go to the repair shop, and I told him so.

But he couldn't stop. He was consumed with solving my problem. He continued to fiddle with the thing, determined to make it work. Other customers needed help by now, the woman attendant was uncomfortable and I was impatient, but he was in another world. Then I remembered how men love to solve problems for women. This man was simply doing his manly thing. I realised I needed to acknowledge this fact in a graceful manner, rather than pursue the other option brewing in my mind — wait for a chance to snatch the item back. So I told this fellow how pleased I was he had been so successful eliminating all of the obvious problems. The repair shop would now be able to proceed so much more quickly. He looked up at me, smiled and handed it back.

If you now combine this penchant for problem-solving with his need to produce, you will get a thing called *functionality*. The highest forms of functionality are probably the branches of the military, those organisations which operate at high levels of efficiency and effectiveness. Such a functional enterprise approximates the operations of a well running machine. Little wonder — functionality is the same machinery as men's minds. Is there something wrong with this machine-like functionality? Not a bit. Machinery is clear, clean, efficient and extremely useful. It's just a bit mechanical. And unintelligent.

The one-trick pony

So early on here, we have to confirm a suspicion you may have had from time to time. Men are stupid. Relative to women's minds, men's minds are not with the programme. Your authors are aware that the word "stupid" sounds extreme. But we mean it. Your man's brain is extremely logical, linear and problem-solving, but it is limited. Women's brains are a great deal more complex and multi-faceted. They are able to operate at much higher levels of sophistication, tolerating and processing a broad range of diverse information.

Before we delve further into this particular feature of men and women, however, we have to emphasise something: if a man is not winning and producing, he is losing. He has no middle ground. He cannot hover somewhere between win and lose. We're sorry you had to wait so long to find this out, but that's it on men. Of course, some may think this description robs men of their "dignity". Men have to be more *complicated*, you know. We actually feel that men have tremendous dignity, but it is not dignity born of complexity. Men are one-trick (well, two-trick) ponies. Winning and producing are everything.

Something else follows from this, however: men will go where they win. This is where you come in. We don't care how many inches you have on your thighs, how great your clothes look, if the features of your face are arranged so that they resemble magazine models, or if you're old or young or blonde or bald … if your man is winning with you, you will have no problems with him.

Maureen: *Princess on the hill, part I*

My client Tony had a crush on a woman named Rebecca. She, on the other hand, was taken with his success in business and wanted him to teach her to do the same. Rebecca appreciated him so much, Tony was very willing. So she came up with an idea to invest with Tony in a fixer-upper. I was pleased to be their agent, but the house had to be inexpensive enough to accommodate Rebecca's limited down-payment. Still, I talked them into looking at an expensive house on what must be the most beautiful hill in the city.

When she looked out of the window of that house, Rebecca dreamed out loud for a moment: "Boy — I'd feel like a princess if I lived in this house." Tony and I glanced at each other. The next day, he bought the whole thing for her. Rebecca was actually put off by this, because she wanted to establish her competence in a business enterprise, not a romantic one. How-ever, circumstances soon forced her to stay there. And even though he rarely saw her, Tony told me that the few months she made use of his gift were some of the best in his life. Tony was winning by providing what his loved-one wanted. That's all it took.

Princess on the hill, part II

Once upon a time, on the side of a tall mountain, there was a beautiful city occupied only by women. One day, a handsome prince appeared at the gate on a snow-white steed. His armour shone bright in the sun, and a long white plume arched magnificently over his helmet. As his horse snorted and reeled, he shouted to the townswomen, "I have come to marry the princess of this fair city!"

The women were excited with the news and ran to tell the princess in the castle. But when they arrived, she said to the women, "Yes, I saw him. But I don't know … he looks a little silly in that long white plume. Besides, I don't know if he's worthy. Tell him that he must first smite the evil troll that lives under our drawbridge before I will grant him marriage."

So the women told him. Without hesitation, he rode to the castle entrance, found the troll and struggled grimly with it. Finally he smote it and, pulling himself wearily from the castle moat, he proceeded to walk again into the castle to find his princess. When he saw her, he fell to one knee and said, "I have done as you bade me and killed the vile troll. As a gentleman I now ask for your hand, fair princess."

But the princess was startled by his rude intrusion, so she didn't bother to acknowledge the prince's deed. "I'm still not sure of your worthiness," she said. "There is something more you must do."

The prince answered, "Only name it, my princess."

"I want you to kill a dragon 12 leagues from here, and then to bring me the treasure that he stole from me many a year hence."

Silently, and with a wave of his plume, the prince left to perform the deed. A week passed before the city gates again opened to him. In his hands were the princess' treasures — he had defeated the greedy and terrible dragon. So once more he approached the castle. He lay his booty at the feet of the princess and declared, "I have done this deed. The dragon will bother you no more. Now I humbly ask for your hand in marriage."

"So you think that my hand is so easily won?" chirped the princess. "What is so great about this treasure when the army of the next kingdom threatens to take it all away at any moment? If you truly desire my hand, you must destroy this constant peril. Go and prove yourself!" The prince looked up at the princess, and with a nod was off.

Many weeks now passed, and the townswomen were greatly afraid that the prince would fail. But the princess was nonplused and said that if he was indeed worthy, it was the least he could do to defeat this threat to their realm. Finally, the gatekeeper heard the shout of the brave prince beyond the city wall, and everyone, including the princess, watched on as the doors opened to reveal the flag of the defeated army clenched in his fist. "I have done as you wished, fairest princess. Now I beg for your hand."

The townswomen could not contain themselves, and broke into shouts and claps of praise for the noble and courageous warrior. But the princess was not so quick to approve. Instead, she pulled out a scroll and said, "While you were gone, I thought of other things that need to be accomplished before I can really consider you to be worthy. The first one is . . ." But before she could continue, the prince snapped it from her hands.

He gazed for many minutes upon the paper, and as far as his eye could see were more tasks, each one more difficult than the last. And he realised he could never win. So he closed his eyes and reached deeply into his manly soul to find the strength he would need. When he opened his eyes, he looked into the eyes of the princess and said, "Enough of this crap; I'm outta here." (But, of course, *you* would never drive a man to this point.)

The man who fails to win with you will go away; the man who wins with you will stick around. Of course, the degree to which you are pleasured with him is probably the degree to which you're going to let him win. But you shouldn't confuse this with being "nice". Nice is fine when it's genuine. But you are *supposed* to be nice, so nice is sometimes a lie. You know what we mean — you are unhappy with something, but you cover it over by being nice.

But winning is based on something else — the truth. This means that you have discovered those areas where he really is winning with you. And if you are doing this, we guarantee that you will also be getting what you want. Of course, this is the big "if".

We still need to emphasise this point about men and their win/lose machinery: a man will respond fully in any direction that winning occurs. He may not even know consciously that he's winning, but he discovers that everything he touches lately is turning to gold. He becomes energetic, creative and optimistic. Or if he is losing, he cannot figure out why he is slowing down. These two behaviours are perfectly accurate responses to your praise or criticism.

Maureen: *Believe in me*

My previous boyfriend, Joe, called one night and told me he had just lost his main client and had to go bankrupt. Business had been slow everywhere, and he was always grateful to have this particular client who allowed Joe to pay the bills while keeping a staff of 30. Now he not only had to lay off people who were like family to him, but also had a huge mortgage payment and office expenses. He was so overwhelmed that night, I had difficulty even talking to him. He seemed to be in another world.

So I took the bull by the horns. I told him we were going out to our favourite romantic restaurant and drink champagne to new and future challenges, because everything was going to be fine. Because he really didn't know what else to do, he went along with the idea. We actually ended up having a very sensitive and loving evening together. Joe started to trust me like a little boy would his mother.

And then he started to consider that everything would work out perfectly, simply because I was firm, loving and convincing. I believed in him, so he believed in himself instead of doubting his abilities. My reassurance (coupled with my expressed desire to go out and spend money!) instilled enough confidence in him to fly with it. He picked up the threads and today has made an extraordinary comeback.

Production panic

This response to winning or losing is actually the same response that throws men into fits if you express something that you want. Instead of giving him new confidence, as in Maureen's story, expressing your desires can first have the opposite effect. You don't have to be alarmed about it. Just know to expect a thing called "production panic". This happens because your man only wins with you by producing for you. No producing, no winning. Therefore, when you express your desire for something, he typically goes into an instant state of failure to produce that very thing.

It makes no sense at all, but it's true. He goes into immediate losing, immediate testosterone attack. He yells and screams and contradicts and denies and proves his case and expresses grave disappointment in you. Or he scoffs a little, looks down and shakes his head. Or his jaw tightens, and he doesn't say a word. This is all production panic.

A great example of production panic occurs in the classic movie, *The African Queen*. Humphrey Bogart nearly passes out when Katherine Hepburn tries to enrol him in her plan to sink a German battleship. At high volume, and right in her face, he proceeds to list five or six reasons why, "Lady, you're *crazy*!" ... that is, why her desire is so unreasonable. But when Bogart produces, she makes him her hero. When he in turn realises that this feeling of heroism occurs in her presence, he actually falls in love with her.

James: *The man-woman game for this book*

Unfortunately, another example of production panic was in writing this book. Initially I came to Maureen with the purpose of entering into the kind of productive man-woman partnership we've been talking about. It was all very exciting at first, because practically no one has heard of this information, and everyone we ever tell about it is delighted with it. So I was full of high hopes. But soon I found myself scared to death.

I had to produce. I was buried. Comatose. I whined and worried — wrote a little, then worried some more. But we see that the book has been written. How? The only thing which has kept me producing, the only thing which has filled me with the hope and optimism to continue is the energy, support and ongoing series of wins of the two most powerful women I've ever known — my wife and my co-author. My wife, for supporting me despite my rants, and for supporting my alliance with Maureen. And Maureen, for having the ambition to see this book completed right from the start. Neither of these two were flustered during the entire course of the project. That was my role, apparently.

So all you have to do is watch him go berserk, then let him know he will do fine. He will then probably go into a series of smaller production panics, and you can reassure him again. He will eventually start solving the problem.

This is easy to say! Most women stop cold when they get resistance from their man. We will go into this important area later. For now, just hang in there a little longer. Your man is resisting you like crazy, but we swear it's not because he thinks you aren't worth it. It's only because he is panicking.

Yum or yuk

So if you don't back down, are you supposed to keep pushing ahead no matter what he says? You would probably lose respect for your man if he produced whatever you said you wanted no matter what. There may definitely be a place in your life for this kind of perfect servant, but what makes your man more interesting to you is how he will supply feedback on your own desires.

The feedback is usually clear. A man's binary mind typically returns feedback as either "yum" or "yuk", with no grey areas. His emotional response is always one or the other. So how are women supposed to tell the difference between this "yuk" response and the production panic we were just talking about? At first, it may be a little difficult, because most women immediately invalidate themselves, or close up in anger.

But we can mention a couple of indicators. First, production panic has a lot of energy to it, because he is over-reacting to something that actually grabs him in a "yum" way. If something were just "yuk", he would generally not be challenged to produce for it, so he will display less emotion. Another clue is simply to see if he starts acting on your want, or if he mentions it another time. This is usually evidence that at least part of what you expressed is ringing a bell somewhere.

It's all much more complex and interesting than this, because it gets into the whole area of man-woman dialogue, and using your man to gain clarity. Your mind is sophisticated enough to use your man in a quest to discover your own wants. So this is just a teaser for now. The first thing you need to do is find out how powerful that mind of yours is.

Random thought

As we mentioned, your man has a great problem-solving mind, but that's it. His mind will hardly ever deviate from the linear and logical operations required for him to win, produce and solve problems. He loves operating efficiently in his two mental channels. But your mind is like a random-sampling radar interpreting signals on about 12 channels at once. This level of sophistication would paralyse men. It's called "random thought".

Much to many scientists' disappointment, our universe is not very linear. It turns out to be an extremely random and possibly even unknowable place. Reality, as we are finding out, is in its very essence unpredictable and surprising. Of course, scientists try to contain this chaos within boundaries and predictions and so forth, but randomness is the world we live in. So random thought is a great match for reality. It tunes you into all the chaotic and complex relationships of our world. By sampling reality on 12 channels, you are much more able to synthesise and predict trends, directions and strategies.

Researchers have in fact found that the two sides of women's brains are much more intimately linked than men's brains, and that women accordingly process information from both of these domains at once. This may account for your ability to make real-world decisions faster than men, as well as your superior ability to read people's body language, voice tone and facial expressions. The celebrated phenomenon of "women's intuition" is simply this super-sophisticated ability to manage complex observations. Yours is always the big picture. You operate on 12 channels, men on two.

James: *Tuned in*

My wife is a radar. She has an interesting handle on a lot of information, and I haven't a clue where she gets it. When she and I go to a party, in about two minutes, she knows who among the guests is rejecting whom, who is interested in whom, who is confident, who is successful, who is jealous. She seems to synthesise each perspective while all the time evaluating the decor and having an animated conversation with the host. In the same time, I've generally made it to the food table and am looking around for someone to yuk it up with.

The ability to perceive so broadly and insightfully often leaves women watching with disbelief as their men run down the doomed corridors of their tunnel-vision. The kicker is that your twelve channels of random thought also contain linear thinking, but that is only a couple of the channels. As we have seen, women can be expert in any of the traditionally male fields if they choose. But women usually find their other ten channels of perception much more absorbing and enjoyable.

As a result, even women's conversation tends to be richer and more complex than men's. In fact, without the ability of women to tune into men's two linear channels, men and women would probably never talk. So this brings up an important question: how are you ever able to enjoy this man-woman game? The answer is that there is one time when a man gets really smart — when he pays attention to you.

Chapter 5

Women Call; Men Respond

Where you discover the power of your feminine appetite

When a man asks us how to find a girlfriend, we tell him to become involved in something that excites him. Typically, a woman will notice a man who is energetic and excited by what he is doing. Not long after, it occurs to her that he should be channelling this great energy in her direction. At which time she calls him. In *Female Strategies*, Evelyn Shaw states that females of hundreds of species compensate for their limited windows of ovulation by being the sexual aggressors, the ones who call.

Men do not call. Men cannot generate sexual turn-on. Men simply cannot raise their own penis by an act of will (though they would probably give an arm to be able to). Men are only turned on by virtue of their *responses* to women. Part of this response is, of course, men's intense response to visual sexual signals. We humans are fairly unique in that we are upright-standing, front-viewing creatures with hairless skin, all of which heightens the visual response in men. Sweetening the pot more, women have far more sexual indicators on their bodies than any female primate on earth — blushing skin, reddening lips, erect nipples, pronounced curves, even facial expressions betraying emotional and sexual states. Frontal display and exposed skin works for women, too. With sensual touch the most important component of a woman's sexuality, frontal, ex-posed skin, intensifies your already strong responses to tactile stimulation.

Now, unlike other species, good old human freedom of choice is probably all involved with our sexual calling and responding. But don't become too confident here. We humans have developed powerful compensations for the chilling effects that free will might have. Not only front-body exposure, but almost everything else that is even slightly sexual in other primates is vastly extended in us. Whereas most species go into relatively infrequent periods of sexual heat, women experience menstrual "heats" year-round. In addition, women seem to be the only females who experience orgasms — how's that for sexy motivation? Humans also have the longest sexual courtships by far, as well as the longest periods of actual coitus of any primate. All in all, humans are the sexiest primates alive.

Scent-∫uality

In addition, recent studies have discovered that a tiny organ in our nasal cavities responds strongly to a dozen or so chemicals — sexual *pheromones* — produced by human skin. This discovery affirms a link that has previously been shown between our sensitivity to smells and our level of sexual arousal and interest. With our naked skin emitting a profusion of fatty acids, hormones, odours, sebum and sweat, we may be living our lives within a cornucopia of sexual response and communication. Upright walking even implicates armpit odour (also a species first) as a sexual scent. A single woman's armpit odour is at least powerful enough, apparently, to alter the timetables of other women's menstruations.

The scent connection also goes the other way. In many species, male pheromones will operate as aphrodisiacs for females, affecting things like heat cycles. Accordingly, women who spend much time around men will often find their menstrual cycles becoming shorter and more frequent, making their "windows of ovulation" more available for conception. Higher levels of oestrogen preceding menstruation may also play a part by increasing women's sensitivity to male pheromones. Women are the ones with the superior sense of smell anyway, and this corresponds to Ms Shaw's theory that women have such finer discernment in order to pick out healthy males. In any case, after this initial dance of the scents, female pheromones will kick in to announce sexual readiness — they call the male to copulation.

With your skin sustaining nearly double the scent (apocrine) glands of men, you would certainly have an advantage in generating such a "chemistry" of a man's response to you. Yet because a man's ability to register this chemistry is not as sensitive as a woman's, your scent, though abundant, may operate most effectively as a subconscious impression. Maureen, for one, claims that, no matter which of four perfumes she chooses to wear, men always compliment her highly on them. Either she happens to have exceptional skill selecting perfume, or it is her own subliminal pheromones that these men are responding to. The pheromone connection would also explain why turn-on seems to be so *indiscriminate*. A man can find himself entranced with a young woman in the grocery store line, but it's the 60-year old woman behind her, at the right place in her cycle, who is generating the turn-on.

Of course, since we're on the subject, we need only look to the wide variety of perfumes available today to appreciate the huge demand for body scents. The big money is now being spent trying to find the one magical chemical that will comprise the elusive elixir of love. Everyone wants the one miraculous chemical which will stop people in their tracks and make them copulate with the first piece of furniture within reach. Yet the laboratories may be making a mistake by looking for a single substance.

Human physiology is more complex than this. Our immune systems, for one example, pattern their incredibly complex activities from a direct chemical communication with the neurons of our brains, and accordingly seem to mirror and encode our brain's states. Similarly, your sexual call may inspire a complex and balanced "bouquet" of chemicals and scent. And with our human sexuality so intensified, prolonged and elaborated by our sophisticated minds, such a bouquet may go much farther than scent. It may be a complicated, interacting concoction of scent, voice tone, physical reactions, cultural cues, sense of humour, hair colour, way of wrinkling your nose and, no doubt, pure telepathy.

Even though the science of scent-suality is still in its infancy, magic chemicals will never be able to turn you into a sensual siren. Instead, *you* are going to do that. Forget the thrilling scientific complexity of it all. When the chips are down, you can always broadcast your sexual call with grace, inspiration and accuracy.

Maureen: *The source of impotence*

Dorian was a rich, 30-year-old alcoholic when he left his wife. His wife hated his binges and toward the end of their marriage regularly criticised him. The real reason Dorian left was that he couldn't get turned on with her any more. Yet he still loved her, so he wondered if there was something wrong with his manhood. But when he later met Molly, a younger woman, he was relieved to be getting erections again. "All I needed was a younger woman," he thought.

Molly was impressed with Dorian, a wealthy, attractive *bon vivant*. But she didn't know how tired she would get with his alcoholic bouts, and the irresponsibility and childishness that went with them. By this time, Dorian's desire for her also seemed to diminish. But now he knew what was really going on. All the doctors knew what it was: he had ruined his body with alcohol, and he was permanently, physically dysfunctional.

Dorian was devastated. He would never be able to make love to a woman again — at least not with a hard penis. Desperate, he scheduled a penile implant for himself in Europe. But en route for this operation, he met a saleswoman on the plane, this time a couple of years older than he was. They found each other exciting, so after a date that same evening, she invited him up to her suite. Within twenty minutes, Dorian was amazed to find himself with a full-blown erection after two years of debilitating impotence.

Even though this woman was not interested in a lasting

relationship, it didn't stop Dorian from following her madly from country to country, convinced that she and only she could raise the dead. She liked Dorian and still desired him, but also had other lovers at the time and wanted to keep it that way. It didn't bother Dorian — when he was with her, he was a winner.

Molly had found it impossible to give this man wins for very long, so she may have stumbled here. She could have got what she wanted, but she hadn't insisted on it, so she was unable to let him win for providing it. Instead, she just criticised him and they both lost out.

Dire straits and strippers

Men and women have been misled about impotency. Here is the big climb-the-mountain-and-ask-the-guru answer: women are the source of sex. Men do not call. A man cannot raise his penis by an act of will. A man's erection is a matter of *response*. The reason for male impotence, other than something organic, is almost always that the woman doesn't want his erection. A woman may be angry at him (could this be for always taking care of his orgasm, not hers?); or she may not have received enough attention from him that she is ready for his erection. Or she may simply not want the old in-and-out this time around. Perfectly legitimate. As we'll see later, there isn't necessarily a big incentive for women to want traditional intercourse.

However, if some men want to turn this into a way to "blame" women for their impotence, well, we suppose they could — but the point they're making is ridiculous. Either you get what you want, or nobody wins — not because you have a bad attitude, but because you are the source of it all in the first place. If you and your body don't want his erection, then all you have to do is find out what you do want. In other words, keep going for your pleasure, because eventually you'll know exactly what you want from your man. Sex is a completely natural and automatic activity — if you get what you want. If you're not at the place where his erection is useful to you, you don't have to have it.

Obviously, the question of rape arises at this point. Rape

seems to be rather an inversion of impotence: this time, the man has an erection despite the woman's obviously rejecting him. This is a sensitive and difficult subject, and we will discuss it in more detail later. It has to do with something called sexual "tumescence", as well as with something called "being at effect" sexually. Until then, realise that the sexual calling of women can never be twisted into a defence for rape. Did she "really" want sex, or did she "really" not? That is *nobody's* determination but the woman involved. The bottom line on rape is that if a woman says no, a man either stops his advances, or he should probably be shot.

But call and response is still the primary dynamic of men and women. Though seemingly unbeknownst to them, the reason even Masters and Johnson therapies always require the presence of a female partner right from the start is because impotency is all about his *response* to her. Masturbating by himself isn't going to help his ability to perform with a woman. Without the woman being involved, these sessions wouldn't have a chance. On the other hand, *women* who are not experiencing orgasms have remarkable success performing assigned stimulation exercises by themselves. A responder needs his source, but a source only needs herself.

Until recently, the very gradual drop in male testosterone levels after age 40 was thought to have a noticeable influence on male sexual desire. But it turns out it has little independent effect on a man's sexuality. Most researchers agree that the primary causes of male impotence are psychological. Impotence is indeed psychological in a specific way: a man who doubts himself when he is impotent once with a woman can experience anxiety attacks every time after. Such bouts consist of his focusing all of his attention on himself, which is definitely not where it's at (no turn-on there, we have to say). Whatever the reason a man is cut off from his woman, whether it be his fear or her anger, he is cut off from his sexual source.

In the same way, women can often appreciate a man's physique, but they won't *derive turn-on* from that physique. Experiments with pupil-dilation show both men and women responding to pictures of naked women, not to pictures of naked men. Women comprise the tiniest part of *Playgirl* Magazine's readership; gay men comprise the most. Yet both men and women enjoy women's magazines, women's upmarket clothing catalogues and sometimes even magazines such as *Playboy*, because these feature *women* in romantic and sexy circumstances. Sex sells. Women's magazines do not attract women buyers by putting male models on their covers. They attract their buyers by featuring women.

So penises, when soft, typically don't excite you. Erect penises, muscular bums and broad shoulders generally do, however, because these represent what you can do with them, how you can use them. It is still you who envisions putting them to use. For Maureen, the pleasure in watching Polynesian male dancers is for this same reason: the turn-on in the intense movements and postures of these men is the sense of their being willing to please, of their showing off what they can do for her, what they can produce for her.

Have you ever seen men watching a woman stripper when she's particularly seductive and nasty? At first, of course, they are bowled over with their responses to such a woman. Yet after a short time, they are found sitting motionless, as if on tilt, with eyes wide and grins frozen, mechanically producing dollar bills from their pockets.

On the other hand, have you ever seen women watching male strippers? At first, they are generally sedate, almost as if taking time to warm up. But soon, you find they are screaming, yelling, clapping, jumping, standing on their chairs and pushing each other out of the way to get their dollar bills to that man. This is not the simple on/off response of men. This is the process of generation.

Maureen: *The new way*

Remember our discussion about men complimenting me on my perfume no matter which one I'm wearing? Look, it isn't some mysterious pheromone of mine. Ultimately it may be a pheromone, I suppose, but it isn't mysterious. These men are responding to *me*. They are responding to my inner self when I am being pleasured. If anything were to create a magical sexual scent, this would be it — putting pleasure first. When you put your pleasure first, you'll have all the super-scent you need. Plus you'll be happy and five times as sexy for all that.

This happiness even relates to the perfume. Do I put on perfume to attract men? Not at all. I put on perfume for my own pleasure, my own enjoyment. I sense how I am feeling in the morning, and I choose which one of four perfumes fits my mood. Throughout the day, that perfume makes *me* happy. It is my own pleasure which is being nurtured here, and that is what attracts men.

So I don't do things the old way any more. I don't get wrapped up in fear about finding the right man at the right time. I don't try to figure out how I can meet some man, or give him come-on signals, or exchange business cards. I certainly don't do dating seminars. Instead, I go deep within myself, into my own feminine sensuality, confidence and self-appreciation, and I turn myself on for me. After that, I don't have to figure anything out. I don't have a clue how they know, but men show up out of nowhere. The right men always show up.

Yet you may not know right now how to duplicate this little scenario of Maureen's. The place to start is with your own body. Women become turned on to themselves by first responding to their own bodies. If you haven't found this out, do so now. You are both generator and responder to your own sexiness. All you have to do to be a smouldering sensation at work is wear sexy panties that day. Nobody knows about them but you, but coworkers somehow seem to respond to you differently. Get the picture? You are the one generating.

Maureen: *Women are the hunters*

At one time I had an apartment on the edge of town near the border of a red light district. Because of limited parking, I was forced to rent a space right in the midst of "prostitute row". At

54

first, it was uncomfortable as each morning and evening I would be dressed in my corporate clothes walking past these women. I was a fish out of water. I could smell the women's perfume yards away and found myself both fascinated and disgusted with their over and under-dressing, their hair-dos and their junk jewellery. I was also angry at them, because I thought they looked like a mockery of women. After a while, however, I became intrigued with them, and with the men in glamorous cars who would drive by to peruse these ladies.

These women were "putting it out there", and I realised that some of my anger actually came from my own dreariness, for I looked almost asexual in comparison. As it happened, Halloween was around the corner, so for fun I decided to dress up as one of these prostitutes. I dragged out an old blonde wig, put on three layers of make-up, pasted a dark mole to my face, squeezed into one of my workout tights, and wriggled into a mini-skirt. Black high heels, a shoulder purse, dangly earrings and gobs of necklaces topped it off. I even took on the mannerisms of those women I had seen. I couldn't have been more tasteless and tacky if I had tried. I looked like a hooker and started to feel like one, too.

So did anyone like the costume? Let me tell you, I was amazed at how many men were bowled over. It was a shock to discover how many men — no matter whether they fit into categories of "sleazy" or "classy" or just "ordinary" — were drooling over me. I really learned something that night. Men respond to women who are out there, who are not afraid, and who are not hiding from their sexuality.

Women call, men respond. Men must have a woman to be turned on. A man may find himself absorbed in an arousing fantasy, but he cannot generate turn-on directly. He can only respond. Whether it be fantasies, pictures, or the genuine article, a man can only respond to a woman.

What about gay men? Gay men certainly get erections, so what are they responding to? It's a natural enough question, but you should know that understanding the dynamics of a gay male relationship probably isn't going to be of much use to you. Plus, we don't claim any great expertise in the gay world. Our book is for heterosexual relationships, and specifically for the women in them. Until someone gay wants to talk about the sexual dynamics operating in his or her relationships, we would only be guessing.

Nonetheless, it is still women who are the source of sexuality. Even gay relationships must ultimately derive their turn-on from a no-kidding biological woman. Women turn men on; women turn women on; women turn everyone on. Women and men, gay or straight, look at sensuous, attractive, turned-on women and every one of them gets a shot of sensuality from them. Gay men often love to hang around flirtatious, turned-on women, and they'll be the first to admit it. Sensual women are the ones with chutzpah — they're alive and exciting. Maureen cannot get turned on looking at pictures of male hunks. She gets turned on and inspired looking at beautiful, alive, passionate women with great hair, in the best clothes, flaunting their sexuality. It energises her and stimulates her to go for more.

Animal magnetism

This is why keeping your man around can be such an issue. The turn-on of other women is necessarily powerful. Ever run into this rude awakening at a social event? You thought you could take it easy, and then you notice your man across the room being ever so animated and wonderful with some other woman. Of course, for his part, he doesn't have a clue what is happening. After all, he claims, he is having too much fun to be caught up in something as cold and calculating as being reeled in! She really is just interested in his job, and so on.

But this is just two-channel awareness versus twelve. Women are quickly savvy to the calling of other women. On the other hand, maybe you should thank your stars that he is so easy, and that he does just operate on two mental channels. If he had the sophistication of women, you may not have been able to call him in the first place. Your call, like the call of the other woman, is effective because it operates outside his channels.

But it doesn't have to. It can also be expressed directly. For instance, a somewhat obese and homely woman we met had pretty much given up on the possibility of intimacy with men. But when she heard this information about who it is that calls, a light bulb went on. She placed a personal ad that said, "I am fat and ugly. I will be in the café at Young and Ward from 10:00 am to 3:00 pm on weekends. I am visible from the street. If you like what you see, come in and introduce yourself. If you don't, just keep on walking." Did it work? This woman got more action than she could believe. (Plus one proposal. She turned him down.)

With the nature of men being only to respond, your call is powerful, whether direct or indirect. Yet it is much more than a call to sex. Calling places you in a position of power in many ways. Some people, of course, have claimed that "behind every powerful man is a powerful woman" — that women are the "driving force" behind men. In a sense this is true, but women are more accurately the driving *appetite* behind men. Appetite — your essential desires taken as a whole — is the power.

Maureen: *Pleasure and power*

My once-boyfriend Dan was a real case. He was a miser, really, even though he had plenty of money. He would buy clothes and wear them for ever, or would repair his car for 20 years rather than get another. I remember one day he complained that his Bulova watch had broken for the third time. I asked how long he had owned it — twelve years. "Hmm — let me take a look at it." He handed it to me, and I threw it in the trash. I grabbed him and said, "We're going to buy a new one."

A little in shock, he timidly agreed, so I took him to the most expensive place I knew. I quietly told the salesperson to bring out the best watch she had. When the Piajet sparkled diamonds and gold from the black velvet pillow, Dan was paralysed. "It's not my colour," he said.

But I didn't listen. "How much is it?" I asked.

"It's on sale today, ma'am. The regular price is $47,000, but today it's going for $23,000."

Dan looked at me as though I were insane. At the next store, however, we did find one that looked and felt right. It was $2500, still far beyond Dan's comfort zone. He had the money; he just didn't have the comfort zone. He did everything he could to make less expensive watches look and feel good, but he and I knew that the jig was up. Luckily, I had stretched him a bit with the Piajet, so he finally went for the watch we both liked.

He later told me that buying that watch was one of the best things that ever happened to him. Even though I was exhausted by the experience, I could clearly see my power operating. I was delighted for him. The next day, wearing his new watch, he signed up a very lucrative client whom he didn't think he had a chance with. Did the watch close the deal? No. I closed the deal. I empowered my man, and he knew it.

Working up your appetite

When most of us hear the word "power", we generally think of "force". But these two things are different. If you happen to be a *forceful* type of woman, that's not a problem. We're just saying that we are using these two particular words in very different ways. For us, "force" is not power. Force is directed outward. It is exerted over someone, or against someone. But "power" comes as a result of your own personal appetite, basically your desires, so it is directed *back to you* — in the exact opposite direction.

So if you are unnaturally struggling to be some kind of *force* in your man's life, it will make you both crazy. But if you take care of your own appetite, your man will provide all the force you'll ever need. There are a couple of points that go with this, but generally all you have to do is be in touch with your appetite and wants. You are the one who defines the need, the one who defines the want, the one who calls. This is actually the basis of your desire to be attractive. Attraction is pure power … naturally.

When women doubt themselves

Studies show that both men and women seem to enjoy the same levels of humour, with maybe a few differences in style. But whereas men are generally able to take kidding about their appearance, the same thing is decidedly not true about women. We learned that when men doubt themselves, they doubt their production. But *when women doubt themselves, they doubt their attractiveness.*

These two reinforcing each other is even worse, a perfect recipe for a losing relationship. The man is doubting his performance, his ability to produce for his woman, and the woman is doubting her attractiveness, her ability to inspire him. So let's consider your desire to be attractive. It is no mystery that in women's magazines, for instance, almost every advertisement seems to fall into one category: it advertises products which enhance beauty.

Now one idea put forth recently is that this desire for attractiveness is inspired by male society's obsessive insistence on beauty, as Naomi Wolf claims in *The Beauty Myth* (Morrow, 1991). Ms Wolf is an intelligent and conscientious scholar. She looks around and sees women invalidating themselves with men's (and women's) compulsive responses to ideal beauty. She also sees how male society closes doors to women on this basis. She does acknowledge that "people" want to look attractive, so beauty-seeking isn't completely a matter of social conditioning. But she feels that the *imbalance* of this beauty-seeking towards the side of women is the result of conditioning.

Other feminists go further: they believe that lavish purchases of perfumes and cosmetics are not motivated by positive desires to look attractive. Rather, a painful mix of embarrassment and desperation drives women to scent their bodies and paint their faces. Feminine beauty-seeking is thus a rather depressing sham associated with women's oppression, and women must be freed from the tight confines of such man-sanctioned appearances and behaviours. Though some of this may be true, there is a problem with these analyses. These negative renderings of women's motivations are suspiciously pain-oriented. Ms Wolf and these feminists have completely ignored pleasure.

An example may be useful. Our friend Amelia became a successful lawyer because her parents wanted her to, but she hated it. She was hostile and depressed even though she achieved a fair degree of success. Recently, however, she has begun writing children's books for a local publisher and enjoys it so much she's made it her part-time work, even though she's losing some money on the deal.

But what about that legal career? She pursued it out of intense expectations from her parents, but do male expectations of feminine beauty create the same kind of discontent? No. Whereas successful Amelia hated her work, "successfully attractive" women generally seem quite happy about it. They do not long for a chance to be unattractive in life. Here and there for a change, maybe, but not much.

As with Amelia, repressing one's natural desires and behaviours is not very pleasurable. It is painful, frustrating and often self-destructive. Such programming results in an unsatisfying desperation, an itch that never gets scratched. We know that women have had the largest share of such experiences: women who repress their natural aggressiveness, for instance, may find it surfacing later in painful, negative ways.

But it doesn't surface in positive ways. So how do we account for almost all women reporting feelings of real freedom and pleasure when, for instance, they are shopping for clothes, cosmetics and perfumes? It isn't painful repression, but pleasure. One woman, a public speaker, even considers shopping "a spiritual experience". Why? Because shopping is responding to her appetite, and shopping is enhancing her attractiveness. It is the power and pleasure of femininity. Women do not buy billions of dollars' worth of cosmetics and perfumes each year because of repressed desires surfacing in painful obsessions. Women buy these things because it's a pleasure to do so.

Femininity probably equals slavery for some feminists. But

for us, it is power. Claiming that fashion, cosmetics and perfume industries have achieved multi-billion dollar profits because of conditioning actually requires that women be thought of as soft-headed, compliant sheep. We give you more credit than that. Yet it's easy to see how this kind of explanation can take root. If personal pleasure isn't figured into the equation, the only possible explanation left is sinister, painful programming.

Feminine attraction

The desire for attractiveness may have always gone hand-in-hand with human pleasure. Legend has it that a couple of thousand years ago, the Queen Cleopatra noticed specific changes in her appearance after much sexual climaxing. Her skin took on a creamy lustre. Her lips were reddened, her cheeks flushed. Also, there appeared large, dark areas around her eyes which seemed to enhance their beauty and intensity.

The Egyptians already had the custom of applying green pigments to the skin under their eyes. Cleopatra is supposed to have extended this practice to other areas of her face and then exported the practice to Rome. If so, Cleopatra was not trying to conform to a male-maintained ideal of beauty. She was queen of Egypt. She didn't have to conform to anything. Cleopatra was enhancing her own sex. What you are presenting to the world with your cosmetics and perfumes is your sexual call. Enjoy.

Maureen: *Womanhood and transformation*

To describe Carmen would make any feminist proud. She had forty employees under her, and she knew how to control every one of them, man or woman. She was an attractive, efficient, smart, tough woman who had it all together. But after a few years in her work, she was tired of it and wanted to leave. By this time, however, her marriage had also lost its charm. She and her husband were trying to be decent to each other, but soon she was living for the times when he would leave town on business.

Carmen did quit, and then slowly started to undergo a rather amazing transformation. Over a two-year period, she started nourishing herself in a way she never had before. She worked out and bought herself an assortment of nice clothes. She was still interested in the professional world from time to time, however, and would have the odd lunch with Todd, one of her previous staff members. Before, she and Todd had such lunches in order to work out frictions in their business relationship, but now they were friendly. Carmen had never actually figured out their relationship. It seemed to be "love-hate".

But as Carmen became more turned-on to herself, she started putting energy into her own needs that she used to put into fighting men. She started noticing that Todd was attracted to her in a romantic way, and suddenly she sensed a vulnerability she had not experienced before. I also noticed the change. She appeared younger and prettier, and she acted softer and more feminine.

Since this time, Carmen has continued to grow in this femininity. And I have to tell you, I've been fascinated with the whole process. Her previous denial of feminine self-expression has been dissolving before my eyes. It has been one of the most beautiful experiences of my life to see this seemingly tough lady who knew how to castrate any man [see Chapter 6] transform into a soft, youthful, sensuous and desirable woman. She is getting more and more in touch with her own appetite as a woman, and the men are responding everywhere. Brava, Carmen!

Maureen has claimed she remembers sensual feelings at three years of age. She didn't know what they were then, but she remembers the feelings. So we could argue forever whether it is society or genetics that creates a woman's desire to be attractive. But we're not going to insult your intelligence. Instead, it's simply the case, right now in your life. As it stands today, advertisements to which men primarily respond are for computers, socket sets and pickup trucks, and advertisements to which women primarily respond are for "tools" that enhance beauty, desirability and attractiveness. Why tools? Because they are tools which put men to work.

Beyond society's cover stories

The traditional cover story in society, of course, has it that women are pure, demure, angelic flowers interested in "love", who ultimately want nothing more than to snag a man for lifelong marriage, raise a family and teach decent values to their offspring. Men, so the story goes, are the irresponsible sex freaks.

But we challenge this. It's as suspicious as the first time around. Just as Betty Badbitch might be lurking underneath "sugar and spice and all things nice," we also propose that it is the women who are the sex freaks. What are women steered away from in our society? Being loose, sexual, nasty — sex in general. And as with any repressed desire, it soon evolves into the mental equivalent of a hungry dog snarling behind the basement door for satisfaction.

Women naturally want the sexual attention they have been denied. At the same time, however, there are a host of emotional pressures which accompany this sexual tension and have the rather inconvenient habit of making you — at least initially — resistant to sex. We discuss this resistance in detail in later chapters. Until then, try to accept that you typically need a little more time and attention to enjoy the intense sexuality we ascribe to you.

So why don't men need this time? Because they are only *responders*. The overt "lusting after" that seems to be the forte of men is really just the activity of simple response. It is a response that takes over his brain, the simple "yum" of a two-channel man. The magnitude of your sex drive, however, is closer to that of a sleeping tiger — men still catch its scent, but it isn't ferocious until it's awakened. So the fact that you are the "sex freak" doesn't mean that you will be panting and drooling in dark alleyways (on the other hand, it doesn't mean you won't, either). It just means that a tiger who wakes up is definitely something to contend with.

Hopeless romantics

But despite their win-lose, yum-yuk, head-over-heels responses to women, it is men who are the love freaks. What emotions are little boys steered away from? Nurturing, dependence and tenderness. As a result, an adult man walks around in life with a huge barrel of held-in love waiting for someone to dump it on. Men are the hopeless romantics, the traveling minstrels, the ones who write 90 per cent of all romantic poetry and songs. Even university studies show that men are about five times more likely to believe in things like love at first sight, and love overcoming all barriers. They are also more likely than women to say they want to fall in love.

In fact, 25 per cent of all men fall in love on the very first date. Compare this with only 15 per cent of women by the *fourth* date. Women also fall out of love much more quickly than men, whereas men are harder hit by breakups, sometimes taking two to three times as long as women to recover emotionally. Accordingly, the suicide rate among such jilted men is three times that of women. As we might expect, being divorced or widowed also seems to be more devastating for men. Even non-suicide deaths among widowers is higher than for married men, whereas widowed and married *women* fare about the same.

Playboy's Hugh Hefner was recently asked how important it was for him to have had the best of everything over the years. His response was surprising. He claimed that the mansions, the cars, the glamour and *the scene* had not been very important to him. What his life was really about was his search for the romantic ideal, for total empathy and connection with the perfect woman.

Of course, such a romantic connection will probably not horrify the woman involved. But it's not her primary consideration. Instead of women longing for the chance of complete loyalty to Mr Right, more and more women have fantasies about "zipless" encounters that are uninvolved and only sexual. Certainly many women prefer rapport and trust with a man before opening up to him sexually, but many agree that they want this rapport *for the purpose* of opening up to him sexually. So do women ever love? Of course they do. But even when they do fall in love, women don't love in the utterly hopeless way that men do. Women are more practical, with specific needs and specific appetites. Someone said that men are hopeless romantics trying to be powerful and women are powerful, trying to be hopeless romantics. *Men fall in love, but women make deals.*

So what happens if the deal starts to sour? What happens after a man dumps all his held-in love on a woman, then promptly fails to pay her any attention? What happens when this woman's desires are not even heard, much less fulfilled? Easy. Women resort to a time-honoured strategy passed down to them from generation to generation. Castration. Even the nicest women know how to castrate.

Chapter 6

That Satisfying "Plop-Plop"

*Where you learn to recognise castration
and its threat to personal power*

To be fair, men usually deserve it. What would be the major feature of a human being who 1) can only operate on two mental channels, 2) lives in an emotional world of win/lose and 3) is validated and supported by society as being the top dog? What happens when (1) the limitation of his thinking combines with (2) the insecurity of his nature, and these are then mixed in with (3) society's affirmation of how right he is?

The answer is *ego*. The sense of threat and self-righteousness that you may have noticed about your man are the combined effect of his binary soul and his unconditional support by society. Ever experience your man when he is not winning in society? Notice how vulnerable he is when he isn't so right any more? He hasn't really changed; he is still in win/lose. He's just anchored to the "lose" side. Here he can become so depressed and inactive, you may actually find yourself wanting the ego back. He at least seems warm and accessible enough that you probably start telling him how you love him, you know he'll do great, and he's your hero.

As a result of which, old binary switches back to being a winner. Mr Warm-and-Loving once again takes a back seat to Mr Right Ego. So what about when he gets his strokes from society again? There he is, happy-go-lucky, and you are feeling as though you no longer exist. How do you get through to this guy without slapping him on the head?

How to castrate

This is simple. Let out a sigh and look sad. If he talks to you, give him short, muttered, one-word responses. If he asks if anything is wrong, answer, "I'm fine." You can also withdraw sexually. Or you can be more blatant by becoming a criticising "nagger". Or, of course, you can always get on his case at high volume. It's all the same; it's all castration. It's that satisfying "plop-plop".

The vocal approach, like nagging, is called "overt castration". This is similar to the story of the old man who is asked why he constantly beats his donkey over the head: "Before I tell him what to do, I have to get his attention." Overt castration does get his attention, but it might not get it in a desirable way. For instance, you could get it in the form of violence.

The more hidden, quiet approach (sighing, moping) is "covert castration" and will allow you much more safety. However, the only result you usually get from it is somewhat generalised. Your man feels guilty, worried, or generally lousy. For many women, however, this is enough, given the trade-off with personal safety. With covert castration, you are able to communicate, "I'm unhappy," while also communicating, "You're not even up to being my hero — caring enough to listen to me and solve my problem." At the same time, you are forced to hide what you want, so he *can't* do anything about it even if he does hear you. So it's a good triple whammy. Plop-plop … plop.

The best castration, however, is a thing called "blind side" castration. This term is taken from football — the blind-sided tackle. The runner has the ball, he's charging toward the goal line, he sees nothing but an open field ahead, he can almost taste the touchdown. BAM! — he's knocked to the ground by someone who comes out of nowhere. Your man is ambling along in his standard "What, me, worry?" attitude. He's doing just fine, he can see everything lining up dandy. He's a winner, everything is on schedule, everybody is happy. BAM! — you hit him with something that comes out of nowhere.

Blind-siding is a great way to castrate, because it falls somewhere between overt and covert. It is usually overtly expressed, yet the element of surprise generally baffles him so much that he can't register it. He doesn't think to fight back. He just walks around feeling funny for a while until it hits him later. It's almost as good as getting his direct attention, yet all the time you are afforded a safety level close to the more hidden, covert castration.

Whatever the style, these castrations end up "marking" your man. He becomes marked, as in ownership, with a pattern of behaviour that other women will recognise. The marking may reveal itself as a certain non-communicating attitude, a certain expression, a certain posture, a certain obsessiveness — even impotence — for as long as you keep him around, and usually much longer.

Remember Dorian, the hapless alcoholic? A marked man. What better way to mark him as one's own? If he is impotent, he is losing with you but doesn't have the confidence to get free of you. If your man isn't winning with you any more, at least make sure he's losing enough to be catatonic!

Obviously, our discussion about castration is tongue-in-cheek. We wouldn't even mention it except for the fact that it is so often a part of women's strategies for dealing with their men. Sometimes it seems like the only way to get through to that win-lose ego. For example, it seems that every man on this planet is utterly convinced he's a great lover. "I've had no complaints," is a standard, obtuse line. Little does he know that women have probably lied to him. Women do lie. How do you tell some guy that he's lousy in bed? On the other hand, how do you ever get him to improve? Is there an alternative to lying?

Maureen: *Youth and ignorance*

I remember dating a young man I considered perfectly charming. He was fun, good-looking and successful. Our courtship intensified to a point where I found myself imagining that

68

intercourse with him, if and when the moment was right, would be wonderful. Boy, was I wrong! As it turns out, since he was younger than I, he thought he was doing me a favour. He thought I would be enthralled with his ability to get hard quickly and perform without even checking in occasionally to find out if I was happy, dead or alive.

I was shocked when he ended gleefully, with full satisfaction, before I even began to experience a wisp of sensuality. Apparently women had allowed him to get away with this for years. He could ride along on his looks and money and never learn how to make love to a woman. After that performance, he sure wasn't going to learn from me.

Slowly, quietly, seethingly, I asked him to leave and, one more thing: in future, could he some day learn how to please a woman? I remember the precious look on his face — stunned, innocent, disbelieving. Self-centred arrogance bit the dust. I know in retrospect it probably only made him more stupid, but in this situation, it felt right to deliver a well placed castration. That ego needed it.

Men are stupid and *women are mean*. Women are an extremely intelligent part of humanity who provide all the inspiration and appetite for pleasure and progress. But when women are ignored by men, or they encounter men's arrogance, or men's plain *deafness*, women castrate. However, the sense of ownership you may gain by having a "marked man" is fine as far as it goes, but we intend to propose something else that is much more effective, pleasurable and fun. This and the following chapters will lay the foundation for a whole new way of operating with your man, such that everyone gets what they want. Because if you continue to castrate, you will flush your relationship down the toilet.

Maureen: *Dangerous temptation*

I know castration is tempting. But if I were to blister every man I met the way I did that young fellow, I would have few men friends. The ones I did have would be pathetic. Castration doesn't work. When a man in a relationship never seems to please his woman, or seems to do things wrong constantly, you know right away he is being castrated. His woman has often turned into a nagger, with the result that he has stopped communicating. He becomes a puppet just to get her off his back. He also stops being fun, creative, and spontaneous because he feels he will never please her anyway. Castration just buries him, and it buries the relationship.

A two-edged sword

There is another problem with castration: after a while, it cuts both ways. It ends up turning on you and robbing you of your power. If you are angry enough to castrate (and who isn't?), you have obviously been wronged at some time in your life. But in order to castrate continuously, you have to convince yourself that you have no power over being wronged. You literally have to cast yourself in the *role* of being wronged.

Of course, you have been wronged in all likelihood. But you've made some choices by now, and this is where you stand by them. Early in this book, you chose to go for pleasure in your life. And then you chose to go beyond the blame and negativity that has infected man-woman relationships. You can bow out now, but here's the first chance you have to make good on your word.

Women are powerful

You'll first need to remember our little secret — women are powerful. This is the power Maureen recognises when a woman influences her man to "do things wrong constantly," or be a non-communicating, no-fun puppet. But you might object: "Aren't men the powerful ones? Aren't they the top dogs, the ruling class, even the physically stronger of the two sexes?"

Although men may be the top dog from society's (and their own) point of view, and although they are capable of great force, they do not really operate in the realm of power. Men are always striving for power and so forth, but they do that

70

because they don't have any. They also do it to fulfil the appetites of the women in their lives, generally the wife or mother. *These* are the ones with power. You are the one with power — it is the same as appetite, and it is yours when you attend to your own heart and soul.

Remember our discussion about power versus force? "Power" has nothing to do with the force, threat and violence we sometimes associate with men. Of course, you can be as forceful in your life as you want. We're just saying that the phrase, "claim your power", does not necessarily mean "become more forceful". Force is all about resisting something, fighting something. If you are resisting society and men, you must become forceful to do battle with them. You have to sink to that level and become like them. But power is about you, not them.

So where is this supposed power? Your first source is your own appetite, and every man's need to respond to it. But another source of power is that 12-channel awareness. Your mind has it all over men. You are tuned into a whole spectrum of diverse facets of this world. It is similar, in a way, to the power wielded by a successful politician. The one who remains powerful is the one who is aware of widely diverse needs and interests.

This is the power which results from being tuned in. You are naturally aware of the diverse demands of life, and because you are tuned in to others' needs, your power is naturally *principled.* The fundamental moral idea is based upon treating others as if they were you, something your sophisticated radar does quite well. When one is aware of the needs of the many, the "right" thing results as a matter of course.

So initially, it's important for you to know that your desires are in keeping with what is right and good. Don't hold yourself back because someone has said you're being selfish. That's bunk. "Selfish" is the very best thing you can be, because unless your desires are fulfilled, other people's needs don't have a chance. But once you're getting yours, you will naturally start spreading the joy. When you're rolling in satisfaction, everyone around you benefits. Just get what you want from your man. The rest will follow.

Maureen: *Alcohol, appetite and self-esteem*

This is a "triple-message" story. It's about the power of appetite, the power of self-esteem, and the inherent goodness of women's desires. Philip was a 70-year-old widower of one year when I met him. We became platonic friends, but then I discovered he was an alcoholic who would become incoherent and impossible during three-day binges. I myself grew up in a dysfunctional home with an alcoholic father, and I promised myself I would immediately sever any relationship that had this problem. But I gave Philip one chance. I sat down with him and told him he was an acute alcoholic and needed help. He was indignant and annoyed — no one had ever spoken to him like that before. But because Philip trusted me, he signed up for a rehabilitation programme.

But soon he went on another binge, became obsessed and paranoid, and withdrew from the programme. When he announced this during his last call to me, my reply was, "That's fine, Philip. I must go now. I have a promise to keep. Please don't call me or get in touch with me again." I hung up. He called me and wrote me letters for over a year, but I wasn't even tempted to respond. Then one day, he called and quickly said, "Don't hang up. I'm going into the programme." Fortunately, this time, it was a success. It was four years later — four years of sobriety — that he finally met the woman he wanted to marry.

I was not afraid to end the friendship immediately if I didn't get what I wanted. As a result, I was the only person in this man's 40 years of drinking who made any impact upon his addiction. He responded to my clear desire and was well rewarded.

Impotent rage

What Maureen demonstrated in getting what she wanted is self-esteem. This will start to grow as you get clearer about your own wants. You should know, however, that anger also continues to rear its head as you grow in self-esteem. Maybe it

72

is anger at being duped, or at not being told before how to be powerful in a relationship. It may even be anger at not being "found" as a woman until now. Maybe it feels as though you missed out, or that you made bad choices. Anger at yourself will be the tough one.

We already discussed how anger is a barrier to pleasure. But it turns out that anger is also a barrier to the very self-esteem which is uncovering it. Anger, in fact, turns out to be rooted in powerlessness: "impotent rage" is just this. As with our imaginary opponent of before, anger takes away your ability to be effective. It takes away your ability to get what you want. Anger is forceful, and force certainly feels powerful, but anger is a symptom of the exact opposite — powerlessness.

So are we now saying you should hide your anger so that no one will know you feel frustrated or powerless? No — our point is simply that anger, like castration, cuts both ways. It can initially serve as the first bloom of a new sense of freedom and power, but it quickly turns on you. It becomes the *role* of anger, the role of being wronged, the role of victim.

The anatomy of no-fun

It might work like this. You have been hurt in a relationship before, so you are now a bit fearful — if you feel your man becoming distant, for instance. It must be valid for some reason. Your attempts to find this reason turn into relentless *suspicion*. This can be where the role starts. What was at first an innocent wondering now *gets* to you. Suspicion incriminates you in it, and you begin to have no idea whether you are incredibly perceptive, or nuts.

But suspicion continues dutifully along until it comes up with an answer. When you finally get up the nerve to check out the suspicion with your man, it usually broadcasts as an accusation. He feels attacked, so he fires back with a hurtful strike. You either validate your suspicion, get angry at him, whittle away at your self-esteem, or all three. Fear starts, anger results, and ongoing suspicion casts you in the role of the very victim you wanted to avoid.

73

Many women have certainly been victimised in their lives. That is what being second-class is all about. You are an outsider in a man's world, considered second-class your entire life. You are often degraded and ignored by men, and excluded from male power networks.

Therefore, it is nobody's place to determine who is "justified" in being a victim, and who is possibly only stuck in the role. Neither one may ever be true by itself, or both may be true at different times. But the part we know about is the role. Casting yourself in the role of a victim has a tremendous cost: your life, your relationships, your happiness. Also the happiness of your man and your family. Buy into the victim role, and buy right into helpless anger.

But now you will have a choice — to use your second-class status to justify having a losing relationship, or to make your man a winner and get what you want. To some, this might seem an easy decision. It isn't.

The Drug of choice

Escaping from the angry victim role is as hard as kicking a drug habit. That special cocktail of fear, suspicion and anger has a tighter grip on some of us than heroin ever has over its junkies. Fear and anger both "inject" a physical drug, adrenaline, into our systems, while simultaneously driving the very suspicions which continue to ask and to justify.

The whole effect is addiction. It provides the same deep satisfaction we discussed before with castration, but it frays the edges of one's life away. Even when expressed covertly, your anger destroys relationships and self-esteem. Some evidence says it even works to destroy your physical health.

Don't look to society to support you in kicking this addiction. Society is as addicted to pain and anger as you are. The angry people, the self-righteous people, always get the attention in our society. Feminism won't support you in this, either. Feminism serves the vital purpose of helping you *resist domination*, but this can have the unfortunate result that you are cast in the role of victim in order to get into that resistance.

Choosing is power

But if you can bring yourself to the realisation that the power in your life is right now, not in a particular past when you were hurt or victimised, then for *this one moment* you have found that power. Suddenly, you find you have a choice in the matter. And choice is the exact opposite of "victim". If you're a victim, you see, you have no choice in the matter. So when you choose for yourself, in that moment you drop the role.

But the question comes up, *what* do you choose? Now that you have a sense of what it is like to choose for yourself again, how do you choose to stay free of that victim role? How do you start to build self-esteem? The answer to all these questions has to do with our old friends, pain and pleasure. It turns out that the "Road to Pleasure" consists of taking your attention off the pain, anger and suspicion, and putting it on what you want. How's that for a choice?

It may sound simplistic. Actually, there is a reason why the choice for pleasure and away from anger is so difficult, so close to the bone. For centuries, various religions have explained that when desires are thwarted, we get angry. Not very deep and esoteric, we admit. But your desires are all tangled up in the same place with that anger. So this is where choice always resides: right there, close to the bone, in that tiny gap of human freedom between getting what you want and getting angry. The fundamental choice is either to put your attention on what you want, or get angry for not getting it.

You need to recognise *both* this anger and the ability to go for pleasure. If we had suggested that you somehow just stop getting angry, you still wouldn't get what you want. Or if we had suggested you only pursue your wants, without any awareness that anger might be undermining you, then anger would start to poison your relationships again. But our approach is two-fold, and that detail makes all the difference. You can now be aware of the anger, but in the process you will get what you want.

Waiting for him to change

So what about men? Aren't men always the ones flying off the handle? When they become angry, don't they also cast themselves as powerless victims with no self-respect? Yes, they do. And like women, men generally know that anger is bad, even immature or cowardly. But such information helps them about as much as it does you. It is aggravated in men, however, because their win/lose machinery throws them into a fight/flight straitjacket. Hence, if you are a man reading this, know that you had also better start backing off your anger. Anger is not about being right and powerful — it is about being powerless. It wins you no points. All it does is destroy.

On the other hand, our book is written for women. Speaking to you, then, it's probably a bad idea to wait around for your man to get himself under control. You'll resent him whenever he doesn't, and victim-hood will forever be your second self. In fact, you will be even more justified in it. Anger will always be that gratifying rush of pure poison. So when you can, backing off from anger will cast another vote in favour of yourself. You will start to wean yourself away from the addiction, and you will start to build within you more self-confidence, power and grace.

We don't wish to be pie-in-the-sky here. You will still probably become angry from time to time. The point is simply that anger is all about the world of powerlessness. It is a catch-22 emotion that is both an expression of powerlessness and a *contributor* to powerlessness. So please don't think that we're saying to go beyond anger in order to become moral. If you think you're being moral, you'll just sit around like a lump of good-girl. Instead of this, discover yourself as a sensual, sexy, powerful woman who gets what she wants. You have all the tools you need to go for your pleasure.

The man instruction book

Women with men have been like the average consumer with a VCR. On one side lies the instruction book, on the other complete frustration. You try to programme the VCR, and it never works. You read through the instruction manual over and over, follow it step by step, and it still doesn't work. Or maybe once, miraculously, you get it right. Then every time in the future, you struggle to remember exactly how you did that. You have few solutions left. Put up with the VCR delivering only a couple of things you want, or beat on it until it fails to work at all (at which time, of course, you can throw it out and get another one). Neither of these represent much power or mastery, however. Beating on the machine has a lot of force to it, but it has no mastery.

These days, all that women possess for man-woman instruction is "folklore and uproar" — weird cultural folklore about relationships and a lot of uproar about that folklore. You don't even have an instruction booklet. You have old manuscripts written in different languages and times, and a million people fighting over which ones are right. So we're going to play the part of a salesperson for that VCR and tell you that no matter what the instructions say, you have a good machine there. It's a good working machine. You just need to be empowered. You need to know how to run the damn thing.

Chapter 7

Wanting 101

*Where you validate and revitalise
your ability to want*

What makes ours the ultimate "instruction book" is that it describes what is anyway natural for you. And so our first instruction is as easy as a heartbeat. *Want.* That's it. Just want, and want the way you want to want. Underneath your disappointments and forgotten dreams are your simple, natural desires. These are the most powerful things in the world. They are the fountainhead of all human endeavour and the meaning of life.

But wait — sages and philosophers through the centuries have told us that we should curb our wants and desires, haven't they? We don't think so. Curb our compulsions, possibly. Desires and compulsions are superficially similar. But the crucial difference is that "compulsions" will have you convinced you will be happy when they are fulfilled. Not so with desires. When you naturally desire, you are already happy.

Shopping is a great example. Remember how some said shopping is a compulsion? Well, it isn't a desperate compulsion to get happy. Instead, the *whole experience* of shopping is a pleasure. If you do happen to buy something you want, you do so out of this same pleasure. You have been pleasured up to that point, so the same pleasure continues when you make your purchase. Simple. Not painful compulsion, but a pleasure throughout.

Natural desire is therefore the exact opposite of compulsion. We all know compulsion — that's when we make statements like, "I'll be happy when I get a new car." Or, "I'll be happy when I get married." Or, "When I buy this product, I'll be a little

78

happier." We may not state these things out loud, but we act as if we believe them. When we mortgage present happiness against a hoped-for future, we fall right into compulsion.

Compulsion is part of a pain-oriented society. Society generally considers it selfish, sinful, scheming, unfeminine and mercenary to act on your present wants. So you are trained to forego simple human pleasures for a vague future payoff. Of course, it's perfectly natural to look forward to future events and future happiness from time to time. But the way we do it compulsively, we not only fail to have any pleasure during the wait, we also fail to have any fun when it arrives. The new car, the second honeymoon, the big vacation: more times than not, we have no idea how to let ourselves finally enjoy the pleasure we had hoped for.

By now, you're probably getting a good idea of what pleasure, appetite and desire are all about. Still, although you know you have desires, you may not be certain what that powerful appetite of yours is calling for. Also, you may have some doubts that getting in touch with this appetite is going to be the "big answer" we have been claiming. Three things need to be said about such concerns:

1) in our society, you have been systematically discouraged from viewing your appetite and desires as valuable, whereas we wish to let you know that they are the most valuable things in human civilisation;

2) because your desires have been devalued, you may be out of touch with what they are — they could be buried in the mud of unconsciousness;

3) because your desires have been considered so secondary, you may have had to lie about what you want.

Maureen: *Old strategies of control*

Looking back on my earlier years, I notice how my mother used manipulative methods to get around my father whenever she wanted things. She would tell white lies, like saying she had bought certain clothes in a sale, when it wasn't true. She once bought a new record player without consulting him, because she knew he wouldn't allow it. When he returned home to discover it, she told him it was his birthday gift to her.

On many occasions, she would cover herself by saying to me, "Don't tell your father." As a result, I learned to be afraid of men, and I learned to lie about my wants for many years. Like her, I always made sure that the men in my life thought they made the decisions when, in fact, I was manipulating those decisions. I learned to be dishonest because I thought it was the only way to get what I wanted.

When you learn to lie to get something you want, it's easy to be confused about the next thing you want. Some of you may have handled this issue not by lying, but by closing down — by going to sleep over your wants. In either case, you haven't had support discovering your positive needs and desires. So going for the good and discovering what you want can feel foreign, silly, such a change from the pain, sacrifice and resentment we're all trained in.

But your desires are the things that keep you and your man in joy and passion. They run the show, and they make life worth living. You have such an untapped potential for pleasure and for *good*, for orienting yourself toward the positive. You have such an untapped potential for happiness. All it takes is a little attitude and a whole bunch of appetite.

Maureen: *Speak from the heart*

I cannot share enough about how important it is to know deep down what you really want and then to express that want. I have learned this lesson repeatedly: don't lie about my wants, and don't "go unconscious" about them. One day recently, I was wondering why I felt so dissatisfied with the place I lived in, one of the most desirable little havens anyone could find. It was a beautiful private hideaway sporting a wooden spiral staircase that led up to a lovely, romantic master bedroom looking out upon the ocean.

We had the lease for one year and were grateful for it, since rentals are so scarce in that area. So deep down, I was embarrassed to be wanting something different. It occurred to me as we were driving home. "Do you know what I'd really love?" I said to my man. "I'd love our own home — somewhere I can settle all of my belongings and don't have to think about moving, even a year from now." After I said it, I was sure it was the most absurd thing Geoffrey would have expected to hear, since we had only recently moved in and signed the lease.

So I never thought he would take my desire seriously. But he did. About three weeks later, as a complete surprise to me, he put an offer in on a house nearby. I was so excited, I couldn't stop giving him praise and admiration. But as quickly as I praised him, I began to backtrack, worrying about how we would make payments and worrying about how I was the one who had got us into this mess. But I looked at Geoffrey. He wasn't a bit concerned. He was strong, firm and confident. He was delighted he had done his job well, and he was winning for it. Out of this, he was able to move forward and produce enough to handle the expense. Your man may not be able to buy you a house right now, but whenever he can do right by your wants, you will have made him an absolute hero.

Elements of attraction

Would you like to know the reasons Madonna is a superstar?

1) She demands attention;
2) She is a "material girl";
3) She is sexually super-charged.

She has *appetite*. Even women respond to it. She isn't singing men's hopeless love songs. Instead, she is telling the truth about being a woman. She wants money, she wants sex and she wants attention. In her movie, *Truth or Dare*, when someone suggests they turn the roving camera off, Warren Beatty complains that Madonna wouldn't want to *live* off-camera, much less talk. Smart woman.

But when women take on the role of the hopeless romantic, it doesn't work. For instance, many of the songs Karen Carpenter sang were certainly tuneful and nice. But a woman singing romantic adoration songs about men fails to carry much impact. The song, *Close to You*, for instance, was originally written about a man adoring a woman, but was switched by The Carpenters to a woman adoring a man. It is still pretty, of course, but not exactly "woman-powerful". Many men state that this romantic song, role-reversed as it is, makes them feel strange. It's not inspiring. There is nothing to do except sit around and be cherished by "grateful girlfriend". It is non-sexual and non-motivating.

It is interesting that the lyrics about a man adoring a woman, once reversed, were so compatible with the public image of Karen Carpenter, not exactly the image of a turned-on, powerful woman. She seemed rather the opposite of a Madonna — more like a pining schoolgirl. Karen Carpenter's death from complications of anorectic starvation may be a grim footnote to this. It may be that women suffering with *anorexia nervosa* are holding back their feminine appetites so much that they literally starve.

Maureen: *Guilty and undeserving*

Susan had been married just over a year when she received a small inheritance. She and her husband decided to use it as a down payment for their first house. Susan also earned more money than her husband and seemed to play the major role in providing emotional nourishment to the relationship. Sometimes this is just how it is, of course, and we cannot really judge that. But what Susan did in addition reminds me of *financial anorexia*.

Susan was very feminine and, like many women, wanted the usual clothes and frills. But her husband, Allan, disliked spending money for things he thought were unnecessary. So like many women, she followed a pattern of lying from time to time to get around her husband's control. Although she provided more than her fair share financially, she now found herself feeling guilty for lying. This was a woman who was ridden with guilt about her natural appetite. She suppressed her self-esteem and her power because she had been grossly misinformed about what femininity is. She apparently learned it from her mother — don't we all? But it was debilitating to watch.

If Susan had known how to tell the truth about her desires, and then to tell her man in a way that had him responding and producing, she would have had an exciting, turned-on relationship. Allan would have the drive and confidence to produce whatever his woman desired. Until this happens, however, Susan will be stuck with the miserable strategies that her mother employed. She will struggle with her self-esteem, trying to juice-up a dead relationship by having children, and then struggling to keep it intact after those children leave.

Men love little girls

Susan is a shrivelled little girl in an anti-feminine society. Because men struggle to meet society's intense win-lose production requirements, they are often drawn to such withered cases. The demand is lower, the appetite is safer. Little girls are cute, and often energetic and sexy, but they are primarily safe. Every man is walking around with a big barrel of love for someone and a great fear of production failure. With little girls, men can fall in love without having to confront their fear.

Until a man discovers he is some woman's hero, production panic will be a powerful negative motivator. One woman actually used it in reverse for her own purposes. An obnoxious fellow kept coming on to her at social events. After four instances of this, she finally looked into his eyes and said, "All right. You can come home with me. But you'd better be good." By the end of the evening, he had disappeared. She never saw him again.

Production panic is the same thing that motivates a man's eternal quest for a "reasonable woman". A reasonable woman is also a safe woman. She would only operate reasonably within the two channels he knows. The closest he can come is a little girl. She's not quite reasonable, but at least she's safe. In reality, men don't have a clue what they want. If they did, they would want women who were specifically not reasonable — women who were miraculous, women with appetite.

Maureen: *Age and appetite*

I was sitting with 30 people in a seminar on relationships. An elderly, very wrinkled woman asked what she should do about her husband's mistress. "No wonder he plays around," I thought. "She looks dried up, as if she has no life in her." The teacher's response? "What's wrong with *you*? Why don't you get yourself into a bikini and shake your booty for the old boy?" I was astounded. Maybe, just maybe, regardless of age, weight and looks, men will stay interested when women keep their appetites exciting.

Older women are actually notorious for having sexy appetites. So you have our permission to be slightly less desperate about the growing-old thing. Instead, get your appetite back. If you are in little-girl syndrome (whatever your age) look around and find a woman — young, old, maybe someone famous — who best represents to you femininity, appetite and power, and do everything you can to model her. After all, it can only get better.

Maureen: *Queen for a week*

Later that day, the intuitive genius of this seminar leader was continuing to amaze me. He talked about women's appetites — that women needed to give men problems to solve and then acknowledgment for having done well. He looked at me and said, "See this woman? She could handle six men." I was jolted and embarrassed while the thought of sex with six men whisked through my (and everyone's) mind. But later, I understood. In fact, by the time I got home, I had counted *at least* six men who were already performing for me. I was only intimate with one, but I was enjoying the attention of all of them. One was helping me plan a project, one was giving me free massages, another had volunteered to build a planter for me, and so on.

All it requires is to take care of yourself. My friend Michelle described a wonderful relationship which had lasted from the time she was a little girl. Raymond was married with children, as was she, but whenever they saw each other, they still had strong caring feelings for one another. At some point, during a shaky time in Michelle's marriage, she started doubting her attractiveness a great deal, and wanted to have plastic surgery.

It was expensive, and her husband wouldn't hear of spending the money. Raymond, a doctor, not only paid for the operation, but booked her into the best hospital with the best surgeon, and VIP treatment. The surgery went fine, but what happened during her recuperation was incredible. She was so pleased to have such lavish attention, it snowballed. She first found herself receiving flowers daily from both Raymond and her husband. Then she started receiving flowers and candy from men she barely knew. And then she started receiving cards and flowers from three male patients! I was heartened to see how one nourished woman could keep so many men turned on.

Don't back down

So do you want to work hard, or run six men who will get the job done for you? Let's say you've made your choice. What you want is a year-long trip around the world. You go over to him and lay it out with gusto. He looks at you, scowls, then says something like, "Lady, you're *crazy*!" As we discussed, your tendency at this point is to think that your want is the problem, that it has castrated your man. NO! It has not castrated him. It has simply put him into a full-on production-doubting frenzy. He may be in shock, but he hasn't been castrated. Big difference.

So we don't care what his reaction is — don't back down. The enormity of your appetite may have plunged him underwater gasping for air, but at the same instant, you have made him your hero. You have come to him with something you truly and honestly want, and you have assumed that he is big enough to deliver it. You have buried him, but you have made him.

This is crucial. As we said, this is the point where women usually back down. What you want is unreasonable. Totally nuts and inappropriate. But if he is winning with you, and you honestly want both of you to, say, quit your jobs, move to Africa and raise yaks, he'll do it … eventually. Most women don't believe it. The importance of women's wants has been drained away in this society, and women's self-esteem has been drained away with it.

Self-esteem for young women

Self-esteem is essential. One fantastic movement today is for young women aged nine to twelve. Young women of this age begin seriously to doubt their self-esteem, and their roles and identities in society. This new movement therefore concentrates on reinforcing that these young women are strong, capable, intelligent and important. So far, given our society's emphasis on productivity and functionality, these girls are being reinforced in these important areas.

Yet it has not occurred to anyone also to make available to these girls the self-esteem that comes with femininity, because femininity and appetite are not valued much in our society. Femininity tends to be identified with weakness, whereas your authors are identifying it with power. This movement is still in its infancy, however, and may yet incorporate, as the feminist movement may incorporate, the vital power of women's appetite to run their men. Feminine appetite is just too powerful to ignore.

The ability to express your desires goes hand-in-hand with self-esteem. Yet even if appetite is expressed, some women never give their men a chance to act. Afforded so little self-esteem in this society, many women back away from their desires. Instead of expressing themselves, they squelch themselves and learn to *insinuate*, hint at, half-suggest.

Do you remember covert castration? Hinting around is covert *communication*. Here again, it provides you with safety, but the cost is enormous. The first thing it does is confuse you, so that you don't even know what you want any more. The second thing it does is fail to communicate (this guy is dense — there's no way he is going to hear you hinting around). And the third thing it does is castrate unintentionally: "Oh ... (sigh) ... no. Everything is fine. Just go on without me" (plop-plop). The sigh is the killer. That one sets the hook, because it is nonverbal and insinuated.

The losing relationship

Covert communication actually takes place in his mind in the same space as covert castration. Both are hiding something critical. The problem with communicating covertly is that you not only fail to get what you want, you don't even *express* what you want. Instead of your man responding to you in an attentive way, you are left feeling depressed and angry. This gives him more "lose" signals, slows him down even further, and lo and behold, you have given birth to: THE LOSING RELATIONSHIP!

Your man doubts his ability to produce for you, and you doubt your attractiveness, your ability to inspire him. So let us (please) back up. You went wild, you went out on a limb in an alive, vivacious and stunning way. You didn't hint around — you said it. You want a year-long romantic trip around the world with your man. Good job. If you really want this trip, if this is true for you, he will deliver — one way or another. You can count on it. The man-woman connection is stronger than a drug habit (and stronger than an angry-victim habit). Also more fun, healthy and productive.

He will hold your want close to his heart for ever (we promise you), but initially it may serve to invalidate him. So how do you get there from here? How do you keep him from going under? Simple. Break your desire down into smaller chunks. Instead of the Big Desire, start with the first step. Sit around one night with an atlas, and ask him to join you in dreaming about where you would like to travel some day, if you ever get the money. Or express the desire for a new savings account for a special trip. Or to start a business on the side.

Traditionally, breaking large goals into smaller steps has

made women powerful organisers. They have the Big Desire, but they look out at their man and see only a finite human being, taking one task at a time. So they break it down more expertly than any corporation could generate a flow chart. And more powerfully. Women not only fulfil the form and shell of the plan, they are the living, breathing appetite and fire of the plan at every stage.

So now you have to become some kind of planner? No way. You're already there. This isn't "How-to"; this is "You're-it". Don't get hung up in our descriptions. Your natural desire will be the fuel that fires him. We hate to sprinkle star dust on everyone's suffering, but it just may be that what is natural for you is natural for him, too. A woman who is experiencing her full self-expression has enough sensuality to soften the worst unbending, egotistical man. Even Hugh Hefner broke his vow never to marry again by responding to the call of a woman who knew what she wanted.

The only thing you have to avoid is the consensus all around you that, "No — things aren't set up to work naturally ... relationships are a struggle ... men are jerks ... life is suffering." If anyone suggests these things, run for the door. Your own life is at stake. Let them die with "Life Was Horrible" written on their tombstones. You get to have, "What a gas. I lived to the fullest. And I was in love."

Ringing your chimes

It is also true that you will probably change your mind about what you want. Don't worry about it. Isn't that your prerogative as a woman? As long as your hero knows he's a hero, he'll change with you. In fact, you had better allow yourself to change your mind a lot. This is new information for most women. It almost always involves a process of discovery, and what you once wanted may no longer ring your chimes.

So on this road of self-discovery, what *is* a want that rings your chimes? This is one of the most important questions you can ask. It gets back to our discussion about desires versus compulsions. A compulsion is not really any fun to have, because it promises happiness only if fulfilled. Existing in the present, unfulfilled, it is grim, desperate and dead. It is actually how many people have lived their lives — working hard toward the big retirement. They may reach retirement, but they have been so trained in no-fun by this time that retirement itself is no-fun.

But desires that ring your chimes provide happiness now. They feel good right now. It also turns out that these are the desires which will get fulfilled. In fact, the steps to getting anything you want are simple: 1) enjoy not having it; 2) enjoy the process of getting it; and 3) enjoy getting it.

Remarkably, this process naturally generates the "visualisation" that everyone talks about. You know — visualise something in order to receive it? Guess what? Visualisation is a natural by-product of the happiness you feel having your pleasurable desires, and having them acknowledged by your man. Visualisation attends on your happiness like a lover. It is excited from within by your own pleasure. All very simple, very natural.

So the first thing you see when you look out at your man is that he has to accomplish his task bit by bit. The second thing you see is that as much as you love him or respect him (or want to kick him in the pants), he is nothing but a win/lose machine. Cute and all, but just a hockey puck. Just a machine. This is important — now is the time to remember that he runs on winning. There he sits, watching Tv, reading the paper, putting on his shoes, scratching the dog, whatever. How do you start the process? Give him a win.

How long do I wait?

How much he is winning with you will determine how long he takes to deliver. If he believes you think he's a jerk, he will take a long time. You'll probably think he's being mean, but the real reason is just lack of fuel. "Oh, I forgot." "I didn't think you *really* wanted that." "You wanted that now?" Statements like these usually make women want to punch their men in the stomach. But he's just a machine. Without wins, he's stupid.

In addition to this, male ego is usually certain it can fight off production panic by arguing a woman out of her wants. But this is like trying to prove to someone that they only *think* they're sad, or *think* they're happy. It's as stupid as it gets, but it is what you are dealing with in your man. Plus, your whole life you have lived with an insinuation that your needs and desires are secondary in importance. Because your natural desires have been slighted so often, he has no idea what you go through to express them. So second-class status is no longer empty political talk. It is as real as you. Your needs, desires and sense of "who you are" are on the line every time you express yourself.

And we're telling you to express your wants and give him wins? Are we nuts? It's so much easier to reach for that old friend, castration, the stun-gun of a relationship. Whether you castrate overtly or covertly won't matter. Either way you gum up the machine that is supposed to produce for you. Silence castrates with the same impact as if you shouted insults through a loudspeaker. But it's a dead-end. If you are going to get what you want, he must win. You have two huge realities to deal with: one, he is dense; two, he must win. Nothing is going to get him moving, and nothing is going to keep you two in love and progress unless he wins. Quite a quandary.

A promise to yourself

However, early on, you agreed you would start seeking pleasure, not pain. You chose not to get stuck in blame, criticism and anger. Now you get to choose again. This is the moment of truth. This is the point where you cut all ties with that pain-oriented consensus and soar with your man. This is where you look and find out what is honestly right about your man, what is good about him, and explicitly give him a win for that.

Maureen: *Success with giving wins*

Once a woman is a man's cheerleader, and she is genuinely happy and trains him in a way that he is winning, he will want to please her more and more. It may call for a lot of patience. Take the case of my associate. Paul was the perfect klutz. He would break everything he touched, trip over every carpet, lose the car keys, never hear what people said the first time and forget again when they reminded him. He would wear stained shirts, have patches of beard on his face where he missed shaving, and have long hairs growing out of his ears and nose. A real mess.

Yet this man is brilliant and successful in his work and is in constant demand. On the other hand, I noticed that he had a succession of wives and women who had fallen into the role of being very critical of him. That is, until he met Mary in a workout class. So far, this woman seems able to ignore his clumsiness and enjoy Paul's company for his disposition, gentleness and intelligence.

Essentially, she has found him right for the way he is, and this new experience has inspired Paul to want to please her more. After they moved in together, Mary told me that Paul is simple to keep happy. When Paul does the tiniest thing, like bringing her coffee while she's putting on morning make-up, she always remembers to express how grateful she is.

The transformation in Paul has been incredible: he rarely forgets things now, walks with confidence, dresses well, has his shirts professionally laundered, and must look twenty years younger. Mary says he is also a wonderful lover. Why would he shape up like this? The answer isn't complicated — Mary wants it, and she's willing to find him right so she can continue getting what she wants. For Paul's part, he told me he is the happiest he's been in his life.

You are involved in a very personal process. You are trading dissatisfaction with discovering what you want. You are trading being resentful with finding things right about your man. And you are trading criticism with giving him wins. You are trading pain and anger for pleasure and progress. You may encounter a few common barriers along the way. Although one barrier is really that compulsion to criticise and castrate, another barrier is low self-esteem. Giving wins and saying what you want starts him on the road to producing for you, but high self-esteem will give you permission to have it that good, and to keep it that good.

Therefore, we will now start on your first lesson in high self-esteem. Look around. Take a look at your man. He stays with you for one reason — with you, he is a winner. You are already running him successfully. The one and only thing that your man wants in the universe is a smile on your face. He may have this or that dream or want, but it's worthless compared to seeing a smile on that kisser of yours. Smiling is your natural response to getting what you want. All you need is the self-esteem to be adored. You are not small and powerless. You are the only reason that your man is here. All he wants is to see you smiling.

Chapter 8

The Training Cycle
*Where you combine your new knowledge into
a powerful working system*

We have been sneaking up on the most important principle of all man-woman relationships. When things in your relationship are great, this principle is operating smoothly and naturally. It's called "The Training Cycle". Everywhere you find a working relationship, you will find The Training Cycle. It is the magic interface between your desires and his production. It makes sure your man wins, and it makes sure you get what you want.

The Training Cycle is actually what we've been talking about all along. First, if you want his attention, give him a win. Tell him something he does that genuinely pleases you. Then give him a problem he can solve — ask him for a favour you know he can handle. After he produces what you want, be sure to give him another win for doing that. This last win is an expression of your pleasure with his accomplishment. It can be thanking him or complimenting him.

All this positive behaviour may seem like a recipe for submission. But it isn't. Like many books, we could have told you that being positive is the big answer for your relationship. Sure, it's not a bad idea to be positive, but if this were the whole story, you would become a starved little good-girl, struggling to find your man right while getting nothing out of the deal. On the other hand, we could have suggested you always take care of yourself first — also a good idea, because it requires a little audacity and self-esteem on your part. And your man would start to produce for you. But then he would do it with a lot of argument and resistance, again burying your self-esteem. But

93

The Training Cycle is a master stroke: he gets to win, and you get your appetite into action. The Training Cycle hitches him up and lets both of you fly.

The power-win

It's important to know, however, that even though these "wins" are true for you, they don't *involve* you in them much. This is not your chance to start sharing all about yourself, and definitely not your chance to start saying how hard it is for you. This is the time to keep your attention positively on what you want so that it comes back to you. "I love you" is not exactly giving him a win. It's just saying what you love. It's okay — it will pass, because your man, like all of us, likes to be loved. But as a win, it's vague and confusing: does she love me because it's expected, because she's so easy to please, because she feels worthless and insecure, or because I have a woman who is clear I made her happy?

James: *I love you, too*

I have to insert here that I have no idea how to respond to, "I love you," except to say the same thing back. And this is perfectly fine. My wife and I say this to each other from time to time — it's nurturing. But for The Training Cycle, it's weak. I know I am only win/lose. I don't respond well to my wife's statements that do not have a task or problem attached. If I am also winning, even better. "I love you" isn't going to bring me closer to her if what she really means is "I'm feeling lonely." And "I'm feeling lonely," isn't going to have half as much impact as "I'm feeling lonely — could we spend some time together?" This, in turn becomes super-powerful if it's said like this: "You're so great with me. Could we spend some time together?"

So if you are going to get what you want, we suggest you be powerful about it and make your wins be about him. When you find him right, find some specific feature or behaviour of his. For instance:

- I appreciate that you are bringing in an income for us.
- You are really something to be looking for a job so intensely.
- It's great that you are taking care of the house and kids when I'm working.
- Your hair looks great.
- You are a great father.
- You talk with the children in a really positive way.
- You are really enjoyable to unwind with after work.

We'll tell you no lies

When you think in terms of such specifics, the emphasis stays on your man, not on you. At the same time, it's not a con. That is, you honestly tell him what is good or enjoyable about him. Do not *make up* something you like about your man. Remember your own integrity.

For instance, let's say he's standing there complaining about something, and you are definitely not in a mood to listen to it. Now you're supposed to lie and say how great it is that he's sharing this with you? Wrong. That's what the how-to approach would say. It's yuk, a little-girl routine. It denies your person, buries what you want and brings emotional dishonesty into your relationship. It's also yuk because your man hears you say one thing while feeling another. It becomes instant covert castration without you even meaning it. Instead of this mess, we instead suggest honesty, integrity and self-esteem.

The phrase is "*find* him right", after all. Take a moment and find something that you really do think is right about him. The simple fact that he *trusts* you enough to tell you this stuff might be right. Or if that's a little close to home at the moment, maybe a more general point that you're happy he's your man. You may have to reach that far to be able to live with it honestly. After this, remember to express your appetite, say, to give you some time alone. When he delivers on your desire, give him another win. Don't assume that he "knows" he did the job. He doesn't

95

know squat until he hears it from you. You are the one running this show. Be sure you tell him every time he does good.

Maureen: *Kicking butt and taking numbers*

I don't care what man-woman game you're playing, The Training Cycle is the most powerful, self-esteem-building, pleasure-generating tool on earth. At one time, I was consulting a small sales operation in town. The three salesmen involved all had that high-energy intensity which women generally find infuriating. But they were nothing but win/lose responders, so I made sure the response was to me. Even when they acted like jerks, I always continued to focus on their good points. At the same time, I never let up on giving each one something to do.

As a result, these men produced for me continuously and were as pleased as punch to do it. I regularly had them coming to me for what they called "input" (code word for "praise"). They called me "the whip master", but they also reported they had never had so much fun starting up a new enterprise, and our sales went through the roof. If any one of them started to come around a little too often for "input", I took this as a sign he could handle much more. So I gave it to him.

Once, however, I was reluctant to tell one of them, Hank, that his business plan was inadequate. I kept putting him off, but after he came around for the fourth time, I finally faced it. My first words? "I think some of your work here is fantastic. Your knowledge really comes through." This was true, actually, so I continued to lay it on a bit. But I also didn't miss a beat: "These are the things we're going to need in addition, and these are the things you need to rewrite. Also, by the way, we need the whole plan completed by Wednesday [two days from then]. That's pretty soon, but I know you can do it." I remember Hank as he walked away — he was a champion. He was confident and committed. Whereas he had nearly come to a halt as a result of some criticisms from another salesman, now he was on full throttle.

The only problem occurred when these fellows' women

96

came into the office. The men were so used to catering to my wants, I had to make sure these women were considered first. So I kept directing the men's attention back to them, and making sure they were getting what they wanted. If I hadn't done this, it wouldn't have been long before these ladies would have felt threatened by me.

Fire give me heat

But let's hold on here. Maybe you can see that pleasure and positivity can feel new and foreign, but this part about women's power is revealing a downside. If you're the powerful one, you're also the one who is responsible, right? And if you're the responsible one, you may feel you *have to* run your man this way.

This is a tricky position for us to respond to effectively. It's pure resistance, of course. It includes emotional barriers and past pain and past criticisms and resentment. But we should allow that no, you do not have to do anything that we suggest. You do not have to exercise your power to get what you want. We know what it's like to feel resistance to this information.

Yet you should also know that we aren't going to let up. We're going to continue shouting from the sidelines, encouraging you and taunting you to get what you want from your man. Our solemn promise is that we will continue to be on your case with some powerful incentives.

One incentive is that you will, in fact, start getting what you want from your man. A second is that the pleasure in your relationship will go way up, the anger way down. A third is that your man will fall in love with you again. Probably a fourth is that life will seem simpler, more joyful, more fulfilling. And a fifth incentive is that if you don't get what you want from your man, another woman will.

But even with these motivations, you may want to slip back again into resistance. And nowhere will resistance be more acute than with that first exasperating "win". Maybe you'll give him a win *after* he produces for you. You have a desire for something, and all of a sudden you have to turn around in the exact opposite direction and fill his needs first? No way, you say. It's *unfair*. Why should you always have to prime this pump?

The answer is that you are the only one with the power to initiate the process. You are the one supplying the appetite in the first place. You have to give wood to the fireplace before it gives heat. Anyway, finding him right is never supposed to be against your nature. It should be completely honest for you. If, for instance, you discover you cannot find him right for *anything*, what on earth are you doing with him?

Maureen: *Letting him have the win*

I am proud that I have been enough of a rebel to affirm my own healthy feminine appetite — and to turn my men into strong producers — throughout my life. But in the past, I never knew why my men put up such resistance to me after a while. It made me think I had become less exciting to them, somehow not "good enough". This made me angry that they didn't have the same respect for my desires and intuitions that they should.

For instance, my ex-husband, Bill, complained that he felt not inspired by my wants, but manipulated and tricked. I suppose some of this trickery was learned from my mother. I can remember my father expressing a similar anger. In any case, my appetite became a battleground between my anger that Bill didn't respect my wishes any more, and Bill's anger that he felt manipulated and unappreciated.

This may have been the sticking point: I, too, felt unappreciated — for the creativity and the energy that I brought to our marriage. Before I arrived, for instance, his business was barely making it. By the time I left, it had grown 1000 per cent. And for a long time after I left, it actually shrank. Luckily, Bill is still a responder. Responding to the wants of lovely women in his life today, business is doing fine.

Now I see where it broke down, however. I hadn't the benefit of really knowing about The Training Cycle before, of knowing that Bill was only a win/lose machine. I know I always thanked him when he produced for me — at least at first — but I never thought of finding something right about him before I expressed my wants. I probably felt too meek. Toward the end, of course, I simply didn't want to. Why would I lie about what I thought of him, when he tried to make me feel bad for expressing my desires?

Of course, I now understand that I didn't need to find him right for the thing I hated in him — his resistance to me. But I could have found him right for things I honestly thought were good. I know that my appetite is like rocket fuel, but my wins are oil. All fuel and no oil blows up the machine.

I just didn't know it then. I didn't know how to go for pleasure in a way that worked. But you now know. You may not perform it all perfectly — that's fine. Just keep going. And don't forget The Training Cycle.

Devil may care

Again, this may seem unnatural at first. A pain-oriented society, remember, responds to criticisms, not positive observations. Fix the bad, but leave "well enough" alone. If you find something right, whatever you do, *don't* talk about it, because you will open yourself up for disappointment. Pain-oriented thinking also takes hold when you express your positive appetite. It feels uncomfortable, gross or silly or you feel that your man should be able to read your mind. He should already know what you want! When you were first in love, he knew. He just knew. You're a human being, after all — it's obvious what a human being needs.

We understand that it's better when he already knows. The problem is that it rarely happens any more. Why? Because he is not "a human being" the way you are a human being. He is a win/lose machine, with his win/lose interests currently directed elsewhere. It's not that you aren't his heart-and-soul any more. It's just that he has moved on to other games. Sorry — it's the way his brain is. Just because your appetites are obvious to you

99

doesn't mean they are to him. So don't be afraid to express yourself out loud. You're not going to disappear, we promise. In any case, this entire orientation toward the negative is the first demon tempting you away from a winning relationship.

There is a second demon as well: "retro-feminism" (our word). Women are quite rightly terrified of returning to some of their mother's submissive behaviours around men. "What?" you say, "I'm supposed to become a Pollyanna with nothing but unrealistic praise for this guy? Sure, he's okay, but let's get real here. Should I really let Mr Man-Ego win like this?" Actually, this is the reaction of someone who is angry about having been a little girl. Initially, little girls do nothing but find their men right, yet express no appetite. Years later, they discover they've been cheated in the interchange, so they're angry.

Therefore, this book is specifically not goody two-shoes, submissive, or "retro-feminist". This book leads the way to exercising your powerful appetite, not remaining stuck in the role of a little girl. Angry little girls have problems finding their men right. But women don't. Women are having too much fun. A little girl (of any age) is still tiptoeing around her wants. But a woman is joyfully *ripping hers off.*

Maureen: *Use him or lose him*

Lydia, a really super friend of mine, had a wealthy friend, Jonathan, with a crush on her. Normally, something like this would be just fine, of course, but Jonathan was also a miser. He invited her to dinner, which was nice. But the fact that it was at the lowest-priced restaurant in an otherwise elegant hotel really bugged her. On one level, he wanted to be the hero, the man who could give his date a special experience. But at the same time, he kept sabotaging this sentiment by carefully choosing the cheapest restaurant he could. So I gave Lydia a suggestion: ignore what he did, and instead make the evening *hers.*

Boy, did she! Though she could barely afford it at the time, she went out and bought herself a new outfit just for the occasion. By the time she arrived at dinner, she was glittering with new clothes and a whole new attitude. Jonathan couldn't help admiring how lovely she looked. She told him that she had bought the outfit especially for dinner, but couldn't find the right earrings. "I thought you would buy me some," she said, partly joking.

As expected, Jonathan responded nervously: "They would be too expensive in the shops around here." Lydia said offhandedly, "Costume jewellery doesn't cost that much." To her surprise, he suggested looking for some later. So after dinner, she did find some inexpensive earrings, but Jonathan didn't like them. He looked around the store and spotted another pair, with bracelet to match, under a spotlight in a glass case.

Lydia watched with disbelief as Jonathan asked the saleswoman to get the obviously expensive pieces. When she tried them on, everyone agreed they were perfect. Then came the crunch — Jonathan realised he didn't know the price. "How much will they cost?" he asked. The saleswoman told him, $475.

He was stunned. He just started to say "No" when Lydia, bless her heart, stopped him dead in his tracks. "Jonathan," she said, "stop right now. You've enjoyed buying me this gift so far, and $475 to you is like five dollars to me. Don't rip yourself off from the enjoyment of giving a gift. You are the one who loses by keeping yourself from the pleasure of giving what your heart wants to."

Lydia told me she wished she had a picture of the saleswoman watching with her mouth open. This same woman jumped when Jonathan slapped his hand on the counter. "Wrap it up," he said. As they were leaving, he turned to Lydia and said simply, "Thank you for that." He got the message. Responding to a woman's appetite is one of the greatest pleasures a man can have. It makes him bigger; it makes him a hero; it makes him a man.

Love and generosity

When you are in love — when you are thrilled and turned on, feeling attractive and blessed — doesn't praise for your man come naturally to your lips? There is no thought at that point about who is giving more, who is giving first, how the scales are stacking up. The atmosphere is instead rich with a natural generosity from both of you. This generosity is completely valid. You are not being conned or fooled or ripped off when you experience love. But even though you are in heaven when you are in love, society puts precious little value on such happiness. Therefore, if that winning relationship goes away, that's when you become an emotional accountant adding it all up, and an emotional lawyer figuring out who did more dirt to the other one — who is more of the victim, who is owed the most vengeance.

But winning relationships take this kind of cynicism and blow it out of the window. If you can muster the courage to go for the good again in a way that works, your wish is The Training Cycle's command. Just watch out for the demons. Demon No. 1: society would much rather you whine and complain instead of vocalise what you want and need. Demon No. 2: telling him something right about himself smacks of the submissive woman of the 50s. And now, demon No. 3: we've all been wrecked on the rocks of love, and we remember the pain, so we judge ourselves as being fooled, ripped-off and taken advantage of.

All that really happened back then was that you didn't get what you wanted. He, on the other hand, may have found he won more with someone else. Or with everyone else, in the worst cases. So he didn't win, but neither did you. That's the way it is. Relationships are either win-win or lose-lose. He isn't going to win unless you get what you want. So remember your appetite, or there is little reason even to be in a relationship.

Maureen: *True colours*

Genevieve, a nurse I worked with, used to tell me about her ongoing affair with a man which had lasted an amazing twenty years. Yet Genevieve was perplexed why her man's personality changed drastically in the company of his wife. His marriage seemed to be the old-fashioned kind where the man states what he wants and the woman obeys. In fact, he confessed to Genevieve that he often hated himself for how he acted. He knew his wife was extremely nice and didn't deserve how angry he sometimes became.

But with Genevieve, he was different. He loved to buy her jewellery and clothes and take her to the best places. When away on a weekend skiing trip, he even helped her clean the dishes, something he had never done before in his life. His wife, of course, received none of these caring gestures. Nor had she ever asked for them. In fact, she never seemed to ask for anything for herself, anything to make herself more attractive, or more sensuous, or happier. Apparently, the one expression of appetite which she allowed herself was having children, so she had seven of them. Because she derived all her emotional nourishment from being a good mother, when these children finally left home, she had nothing left. Her husband couldn't stand being around this completely purposeless woman now. He told Genevieve that he wanted to leave his wife and marry her.

Although Genevieve had enough sense, and heart, to turn him down, there is a moral to this story. Men go where they win, and they cannot win where there is no appetite. No appetite, no response, no winning, no relationship. Women, even women like this one, must develop the courage to discover what they want and express those desires. And when their man delivers, they must be willing to praise him for it.

Sometimes, however, you may find yourself holding your praise back, not out of stinginess or anger, but simply out of the sophistication of that mind of yours. That is, because you generally keep your radar operating on many channels at once, it's easy to become bogged down in considerations of "everything". Because there will always be something that isn't quite right or complete, you forget to find your man right for what he *has* produced. You leave him in the lurch because you're on to the next thing.

Yet this is just a problem with 12 channels communicating

with two channels. So whatever you do, don't forget to praise what he has produced so far. Make "win-problem-win" sandwiches and keep on feeding. You'll have so much of his attention on you that your self-esteem will have to quadruple in order to accommodate it (hint).

When your self-esteem grows, you'll find that your personal power also grows. You continue moving from little girl to woman. A little girl doesn't understand why her man becomes angry when she is being nice. There are three reasons: one, she is ignoring her appetite so he won't leave her (this amounts to a no-integrity relationship where her man *can't figure out* if he's winning or losing). Two, she cannot help but castrate non-verbally because she isn't happy. And three, because she is holding back on expressing her appetite, her man is being tragically under-used.

Imagine a prize-winning racehorse forced to remain in a stall all day comfortably eating apples and oats. He'll hang around, because *that* is the one desire his owner is expressing to him. But you have a prize-winning racehorse on your hands! Use him up, or turn him loose to someone else. A little girl hopes that the apples and sugar cubes she's bringing every hour are what he wants. She's hoping he's happy and content. She doesn't understand why he keeps kicking his stall — it's terrifying when this huge animal acts like that. She worries that she isn't making it easy enough.

In the meantime, wind is whipping through a woman's hair. She is in ecstasy, laughing and alive. She is gripping that charging beast with all her strength. Her boot heels are in his flanks, and she's yelling at the top of her lungs, "You beautiful animal — faster! More! *I want more!*"

This is the winning relationship.

Chapter 9

The Road to Clarity

Where you grow in clarity and certainty about your wants, and discover three basic levels of appetite

So let's say you're excited about the possibilities for your new winning relationship. You've made your man right — you've got his attention, and here is your chance. All you need to do is say it. This is the beginning of a great partnership. You don't want to blow it. All you need to do is just go ahead and let him know what you want ... and ... it ... doesn't quite come together.

Did you fail? Not in the least. You're just getting used to this whole approach, after all. It's okay to give yourself a break. But the important thing is to keep going for what you want. An infant starting to walk stands up and falls down over and over. Nobody criticises this little human for falling, and the infant continues naturally to seek its pleasure by standing up again and again. In the area of acknowledging and expressing their desires, however, most women have been stonewalled.

Therefore, the frustration embodied in that familiar question, "What do women want?" is real enough. Men just don't understand that this question comes up because they are the ones who put *zero value* on women's wants in the first place. With your desires all bound up with your self-esteem, and with men panicking every time you express yourself, little wonder that you have trouble getting a handle on what you want from time to time.

The cloth merchant

So kick back and relax for just a moment. Imagine this scenario. You have arrived at a country fair and are interested in buying some fine cloth. A pleasant little man in a beret notices your interest. He greets you with a smile, and asks you if you would like to see some of his coloured cloths. You aren't quite sure if his cloths are what you want. Do you invalidate yourself for being unsure? Of course not. You naturally accept that your sophisticated mental apparatus requires all kinds of data, all kinds of options. How do you go about accepting this abstract notion? *You start to enjoy yourself.* All of the self-acceptance stuff that psychologists want us to achieve sits right there alongside personal pleasure.

So back to the fair. This merchant is a smart fellow. He walks graciously to the front of his stand and starts unfurling one of his bolts. Then he does another. You feel you have all the time in the world. "Isn't this a pretty yellow here?" he asks. He steps back and looks at it. "Do you think it's too bright? Because we also have some blues which may interest you. Or else something dramatic like red? You can feel this fabric — does this feel right, or would you like something finer? Are you thinking of something airy and light, or something more sheer and elegant? How about this one? You like the fabric, but you want to see it in green? How about this green? Too dark. Okay, how about this green? Too washed out? Yes, I see. Okay. How about this lighter blue-green?"

The cloth merchant is your man. If you don't know what you want, the first thing your man gets to produce for you is clarity. It just goes with the territory: 12 channels have a little more difficulty zeroing in on one choice. Whereas two channels are good at arriving at one choice over one other, they generally are unable to consider a range of options simultaneously. Both of you operating together, however, make a winner. It is perfect man-woman dialogue, and it begins with something like this: "Honey? I'm not sure what I want here. You're really great at narrowing things down — can you help me?" He'll be right in your corner.

So he suggests that what you probably want is to lie down and relax for a while. "Good idea, but I don't think that's quite it." Okay, maybe you want to go to a movie? "That's good, too.

But I'm not sure. You're really helping me, though. What else?"
We believe this is the finest discussion a man and woman can have with each other. Your appetite inspires a dialogue where your man wins by discovering what your appetite is. Wow. Once you do get a fix on what you want, you've involved him in such a powerful series of wins and problem-solvings, he will generally be head over heels to deliver it.

You might have simply wanted more attention — if so, you just got it. Or you wanted to go out somewhere. Where? "How about dancing? How about getting together with friends? How about dinner? How about a walk?" Your man will continue to produce for you (with a couple of periods of frustration, possibly, unlike our perfect cloth merchant) *as long as you keep the wins coming.*

On the other hand, your man may come up with something like, "I can't read your mind." Or, "You're going to have to figure that one out on your own." But instead of gritting your teeth and walking away, keep the wins coming. Don't be intimidated. Just tell him how good he is at this, and again express your desire for clarity. Also, no sneaky stuff here. If you already know what you want, don't use this process to fool your man into putting his attention on you. All this does is destroy any respect you have for him. Plus it's too much (unpleasant) work. If you know what you want, find him right, say what you want and give him a win when he produces it.

The first level of appetite — sex

It's important to realise that your man cannot operate blindly. If you didn't have *any* sense of what you want, not even a perfect cloth merchant could help you. You are involving yourself in a very sensitive process here. Not only have you been taught to downplay many of your own wants, the few wants you do recognise may have all kinds of value judgments attached. Therefore, in order to revitalise this whole area, we're going to offer you information about appetite. This information is not designed to pigeonhole your preferences, but to help you back on the path to expressing yourself. There are actually three

107

basic levels of appetite. By "levels", we simply mean levels of importance to you. We'll treat each one in turn.

As you may have fathomed by now, the first and most important level is going to have a lot to do with sex. In fact, it includes all forms of attention to you. Yet this level is still directly sexual and is related to your body's changing level of sexual tension. We cover this area in depth when we discuss sexual "tumescence" in later chapters. But for now, you are doubtless aware of how sexual tension can manifest in various emotional pressures. Such pressures often start seven to ten days before menstruation and, in more exaggerated cases, come under the heading of what some doctors still label "PMS".

But it's nothing that a few orgasms a day won't cure! Of course, in a pain-oriented society, the solution is hormone-blocking chemicals, or even tranquilising drugs. Orgasm? A pleasurable response to a natural condition? We certainly couldn't do that — it would hardly be functional. Wouldn't we be silly, or sick, or go to hell or something? The answer is, No. If you have to take PMS drugs, that's fine. Take as many as you want. But it's nice to know there is also a pleasurable, healthy alternative for you: orgasms will make a world of difference. Although orgasm is the primary "cure" (no prescription has ever tasted so good), all other forms of attention have good effects. Receiving a hug, getting massaged, taking a hot bath — even having a conversation with someone, or receiving a compliment. Each of these small pleasures reduces sexual tension.

A second level of appetite — food

Many of the coming chapters are devoted to the primary level of sex and attention. But we leave it now to talk about other aspects of your appetite that can come into play. When "Sex" is being satisfied, another level usually presents itself called "Food". This includes, obviously, food, but also things like family, stability, home and security. "Food" corresponds roughly to that time of life when a woman is raising a family. But making babies is not necessarily the major drive of this appetite. It can be, and if so, can be as powerful a drive as Sex. But often, Food is oriented toward stability, toward future direction and security. Even so, the grip of children can be a powerful incentive for both sexes.

Maureen: *Believe it or not*

I asked the seminar leader why a man I had been going with for two years suddenly seemed to put me on the back burner. In a wink, all the romance had left. He asked me, "Has he got another woman?"

"I don't think so," I said, "because his son has come to live with him. But I almost feel that the two of them are ganging up on me and making fun of me behind my back."

He didn't miss a beat: "He's still serving and responding to his first woman and the mother of his children ... it's a tough one to get past the one who drops the babies. Besides that, he's gay. Where is your self-esteem? Why don't you tell him good-bye? There's something really wrong with your self-esteem."

As usual with this man, this mentor, I was flabbergasted. First, I discovered that I didn't have a chance to make my needs felt over the woman who bore my lover's children years before. And second, my man was gay? I couldn't believe it. But when I did break up with him later, I found pictures of my ex-lover being intimate with other men.

Aside from the stunner about his being gay, I have been intrigued with this appetite for children, and the hold that it can have over fathers. It is common, for instance, to find women who have children out of a desperate desire to save their marriages. It's a way they can say, "See — I have appetite; I have validity." But it is a primitive and ineffective way to keep their man producing for them. Often what a woman really wants is more depth, bonding or commitment from her man.

Another thing she may want is to drive away jealousy and insecurity. The arrival of a baby anchors her man morally, and apparently biologically. So again, I need to emphasise how important it is to get clear about your wants from the core of your inner self. Children are fine as a natural appetite, but to have them simply in order to validate yourself in this producer-society, or to produce the bonding that you aren't getting — or even to motivate your man to produce more — these are all feeble reasons for creating a family. Do it out of appetite, not out of low self-esteem.

So just as there is enough social confusion about the appetite of Sex, so is there social confusion about this new appetite. That is, out of the vast range of abilities and talents women have, the only one that is recognised in our society is that which manufactures something. In a society built on productivity, the only valid role women know is to be factories and farmers of children. This is why they lean to this when their self-esteem isn't up to par.

Remember the woman with seven children who was at the bad end of her husband's twenty-year affair? Sure she had appetite, but she was underground with it. She couldn't express it for what it was, so she expressed it in the only way supported by society, making babies. But the pleasure of it became less and less until, toward the end, it was nil. As pleasure decreases, the natural power of appetite, which depends on that pleasure, goes out the window.

A third level of appetite — baubles

When you are receiving adequate sex and attention, and after you have established home, security, possibly family, a third level of appetite typically kicks in — "Baubles". In a producer-society, we are generally taught to scorn anything that we believe is not directly functional, as well as to belittle the natural desire of women to look and feel attractive. But women's attractiveness is exactly what "Baubles" are all about. They are in fact defined as unnecessary, unsolicited testaments to a woman's beauty.

They include things like jewellery and fur coats (faux, we hope), but they may also cover things like romantic *soirées* that your man is able to bestow. However, although baubles can nourish you to an extent, they usually don't occupy the *primary* position in the hierarchy of your desires. If you are receiving nothing in the "Sex" column, for example, baubles will be meagre compensation. We've all heard the classic scenario of a man complaining that he "busts his rear" all day only to be castrated by his woman the instant he walks in the door. His woman may have the house, the jewellery, the bank account. What she now wants is *her man*.

Of course, there are always women who will play the Bauble angle exclusively: "Ooh, dahling, I'm just not sure if you have enough money to be my lover." These women are certainly expressing appetite, and this is why men of means are always drooling over them for a chance to win and be acknowledged. But by itself, the appetite is a little empty.

What makes the category of "Baubles" somewhat more significant is that it relates to the areas of status and position. Though some women deny any particular need for social recognition, it seems to surface from time to time. The woman who wears her expensive jewellery is not only enhancing her beauty, but also showing others how favourably her man regards her. Similarly, in some divorce cases, it turns out that the woman involved may have had no sexual appetite for her husband in years, but she still fights the divorce to avoid being "dethroned".

Getting it right

Do these three levels of appetite exhaust the possibilities? Not in the least. A turned-on woman can be passionately involved in all kinds of things. It's just important for her to keep her bearings in those areas which are the most maligned and misunderstood, but still the most pleasurable and powerful: Sex, Food and Baubles. Because of social ignorance in these areas, men rarely have a clue how to serve their women. We already spoke of the woman who has the house and the jewellery, but who wants the sex and attention she's been missing. Her man is completely baffled — he can't figure out why she keeps dropping him to the mat. The reason is simple — he has been prioritising his woman's wants something like this:

Baubles, the most important, and sex, the least important. The very worst thing he can conceive of is to deprive his woman of material things. To have his woman living in a "tar-paper shack" is a man-producer's nightmare. But he fails to understand that the real hierarchy of women's wants is just the opposite:

When sex and attention have been provided, most women will look back and remember how romantic the full moon was when it used to shine through the cracks of the tar-paper. First comes Sex, then the rest. The man who pays attention to his woman will naturally fulfil all three. All he needs do is pay attention.

Misogyny and fog

Once you are in touch with these levels of appetite, the next trick will be to get them into action. And sometimes this can be scary. For one thing, misogynists have criticised women for centuries for having such natural appetites. Sex, Food and Baubles have become respectively sinfulness, manipulation and vanity. These, however, are labels employed by uninspired men. They fail to realise that the power which has generated civilisation is the same primordial force of feminine pleasure that spins itself out into the complex webs of relationship and human community.

Unfortunately, even feminism has dismissed feminine appetite. In this sense, it, too, is "misogynist": it plays down the importance of your femininity and then identifies you only as a competitor in a producer society. Feminism has opened up producer roles for women who choose to pursue them, but it has overlooked the fact that production will not occur without an appetite to inspire it. We promise to come back to this important topic in our later chapter on femininity and dialogue. For now, suffice it to say that when you are listening to the pulse of your own appetite, you are deciphering the heartbeat of all human progress. Knowing your natural appetites helps you read this pulse.

Yet even if you are willing to brave the personal discomfort of finding out and expressing what you want, society will probably still consider you frivolous. In this culture, only if something is a problem is it ever taken seriously. The way it usually goes, you let your desire remain unfulfilled until it becomes such a big problem that he finally notices. Then he realises you are unhappy, so he tries to fix it. But because most of the problem is that he hasn't given you much attention for the past four years, you're probably into payback and vengeance by now and so you make sure he loses. You need to be validated as attractive and exciting, but now he just wants to get away from you because he feels castrated by your unhappiness ... and so on.

The clear use of words

This describes the painful cycle which you will be halting when you start to consider what you want. So it's good to remember how your behaviour has been guided until now. First, a pain-oriented society has trained you to be more interested in what you *don't want.* Second, you are a second-class citizen, so your wants have regularly been downplayed. And third, your appetite has repeatedly been attacked by men when they go into full-blown production terror.

We sympathise with what you're up against when ferreting out your desires and expressing them. But after we sympathise, there you are with your relationship, and there you are with your power, and there we suggest you start exercising that power. Clarity in your expression is the first step. When expressing your wants, forget the subtlety, the hinting. We understand that it feels gross and inelegant to divulge everything you're thinking, wanting and feeling. Implying things, we know, is so much easier and so much classier, but it does not work. Remember that your man is thick. Use words directly and clearly, and be specific about what you want.

James: *Turning it around*

Julie's husband, Kirk, made money in good times and bad. The two of them owned a Ferrari, had a nice house in a pretty part of town and travelled extensively. Even though Julie was something of a "good girl", her power as a woman made itself felt in Kirk's success. She made him feel right, made him feel a winner and gave him the optimism to persevere. So Kirk was a great producer in those areas *he* felt he should win in. He was successful enough that the few wins he received for paying attention to Julie paled in comparison.

Julie is Japanese, so her style was not to contradict her man, but to support him in what he wanted. Her culture did not encourage her to express her own appetite, so she wasn't getting enough attention. She was well on her way to becoming a "dragon lady". Such a woman is so fed up, she comes to the point where she says to herself and the world, *no more Mr Nice Guy.*

Kirk didn't have a clue why Julie was unhappy. He was doing everything right. What else could a woman want? He began to think she was spoiled and selfish, and he concentrated more and more on where he *was* winning — his practice.

Julie started to doubt herself profoundly. Why wasn't her man attracted to her any more? Was she an ugly person that nobody could like? Then she heard this information about expressing her wants. That night, she bought a roll of paper, unfurled a long piece of it and painted in big red letters, "I

WANT MORE SEX." She taped it to the wall over their bed. Men are thick, but even Kirk was able to get it this time.

Even if your man is not winning in society right now, you can't expect to hint around at what you want. Let him know the specific thing you want. Or if you don't know specifically, let him know you want his support in finding it out. Above all, remember to give him wins. He's got to win somewhere. If he's losing in society, and then also starts losing with you, he's being pushed too far. He *will* do something desperate, and it *will* be something destructive.

So say what you want clearly; just remember to give him wins both before you tell him and after he delivers. Nothing else works. You will probably be original, creative and unique in every other way with your man. But don't be creative with these three simple parts: find him right, then give him a problem he can solve, and then give him another win after he solves it.

That certain something

Because we are being so insistent on this little formula, it can easily feel like slavery or stupidity. Feminists might think you're a doormat, and society might think you're a manipulator, but it isn't true. Doormats don't get what they want. Manipulators don't get what they want for very long. The Training Cycle is simply the only thing that expertly runs your man for the benefit of both of you. Use it like a spiritual discipline. This is a religious ritual that really will bring you joy.

Using your man like this is the only way he will ever trust you. He does not need the safety and ease that comes from repressing yourself. Men are the first in danger, not safety. Your man discovers that he can't win anywhere the way he's winning with you, so you start getting more and more of his attention. People start flocking to you like bees to honey, because your relationship has a "certain something". What you will have is delicious pleasure in your lives.

Chapter 10

Aren't We Beyond All This?

Where you consider your doubts, look at a new style of relationship and create your first list of wants

When a female panda goes into heat a couple times a year, a male in the wild who catches her scent will lope at top speed toward her as far as 13 kilometres, not even knowing if she'll accept him when he gets there. He forgets everything in his lazy, easy, idyllic existence and runs off, even though he has zip guarantee of acceptance. But don't we humans have superior intelligences? Haven't we evolved to the point that man-woman relationships are no longer based upon such animal drives? When sexuality does emerge, doesn't it do so in a very limited way — confined to fifteen minutes a week behind closed doors?

Unfortunately, that may be true for many. But for all of our supposedly incidental sexuality, it's interesting to note that our male panda goes bonkers only twice a year — only during a heat. As we found out, women are not limited to a few weeks of sexual heat per year. Women are sexy all twelve months. Men are loping after women year round. Yes, we are civilised humans. But in human relationships, we don't care how "beyond it all" you think you are. Man-woman is p a n d a - m o n i u m.

Maureen: *Appetite and response*

A couple of girlfriends visiting recently were excited about getting out and meeting men. They spruced themselves up to the hilt: they sunbathed, shopped for new clothes, played romantic music and created a very flirtatious mood around the house. Soon after arriving, they were extremely exciting and sensuous. My boyfriend, for one, was certainly enjoying them!

He had agreed to take me to the doctor one morning for some tests, and I was pleased that he was considerate to take time off for this. That same morning, however, the girls were discussing whether to take the bus or a taxi into town. Suddenly my boyfriend came into the bedroom and announced, "Maureen, I'm taking the girls to town so they can go shopping."

I was astounded. I couldn't believe what I was hearing. "You're what? What happened to taking me to the hospital?"

"Oh, I thought you could drive yourself," he replied.

I hit the roof: "Whose man are you? Mine or theirs?" He was really taken by surprise — why was I having such a temper tantrum? He soon relented and honoured his promise to me, but he still has no idea that he was responding automatically to other calls, other appetites. Just a loping panda.

Is it manipulation?

The idea of wild males loping after every post-pubescent girl/ woman might sound intimidating. So it's important to know that you hold all the cards in this game, much to men's displeasure. The greatest fear in a man's life is that he will be manipulated and controlled, that he won't be his own man. Cute, huh? He actually has a good reason to fear this — he's easy. He just doesn't consciously understand that there is *no* being his own man. A man is not a man until he's being used by a woman. He is no man until you make him one.

He knows this at an unconscious level, however. Young men commonly have the fantasy of being seduced by an older woman who trains them sexually. At some level, men want to know how to satisfy a woman. Sex is probably the most direct instance of a woman's appetite. And men want to know how to serve that appetite. So if your man accuses you of manipulating him, smile, tell him he's really smart and say, "My neck hurts a little. Could you give me a massage here? Right there. Yes ...

117

great. That feels great. You're really attentive to me." Manipulation will be the farthest thing from his mind.

Manipulation is what you did before. It is the dishonest option. Being unhappy and not communicating what you want. Being angry and saying, "I'm fine." Insinuating what you want and losing all respect for him. The Training Cycle is a complete 180 degrees different — it is giving honest wins while your man finds himself turned-on and productive. It's funny that we think this positive process is manipulation, but view anger, guilt and unhappiness as somehow "honest". Could this have anything to do with society's orientation toward fixing the bad?

Get the edge

Besides, you can let your man know all about it if you want. Even when he knows you are running *the official self-conscious and completely obvious training cycle*, it still works. Why? Simply because he enjoys the process of being trained by an expert. He loves to produce and get wins. He will take it in any way he can. You'll be thrilled to find out he actually wants nothing more than to please you. You'll be thrilled to know that all he wants is that smile of yours.

We acknowledge that The Training Cycle might be uncomfortable at first. It's embarrassing to go for pleasure. Plus it's scary to express desires *so obviously*. But look — if it were easy, there would be no reason for this book. Everyone would be doing it. You do it, and you have the edge — the first on your block to turn your relationship into a scorcher.

James: *Flipped into ecstasy*

Once women beat past the doubts, fears and anger associated with The Training Cycle, they are often amazed to find out how *easy* their men are. I remember one woman, Carol, who was fighting regularly with her husband, Mark, over sex. They weren't having much of it, in fact. Carol even found herself infuriated when she did manage to have an orgasm with him, because she knew it would be another 4–6 weeks before she would have another.

Certainly a lose-lose situation. She wasn't getting attention, and he was castrated by her obviously-not-thrilled mood a few moments after intercourse. He doubted his ability to produce, and she was completely doubting her attractiveness. These two had reached the place where even fighting and snapping at each other were no longer means of expression. They were now just slowly burning out their love for each other.

When Carol described this to me, she was hopeless. She didn't understand Mark, and she didn't know what was wrong with her. So I told her that Mark is nothing but a win machine. He is not some unfathomably complex mystery, but a one-trick pony. Then I told her about The Training Cycle. She couldn't believe it, but my enthusiasm apparently sold her. Of course, when she thought about finding him right, she got angry remembering all the times she had felt invalidated by him. But she pushed past these feelings and tried my suggestion that night.

The next morning, she couldn't wait to tell me what had happened. There they were in the kitchen, each futzing around in an icy burn of silence. She tried to find something right about him. She noticed his arms as he cut broccoli and remembered she had always liked them. They were sturdy and masculine with black hair on light skin. So she blurted out, "I like your arms."

Silence. Carol panicked a little. More broccoli chopping. "I love your arms."

He stopped. "Hmm?" he muttered, still looking down.

Carol said, "I've always loved your arms."

Mark paused, then smiled just a little. "Thanks," he said quietly.

Seeing the change, Carol continued. "I love how strong they are." And then in a flash of genius, "And how strong they are when you hold me." Now a very long pause. His head dropped slightly. Then came her appetite: "Would you please hold me?" Mark let out a small sigh. He put the knife down, turned, and gave Carol a long embrace.

She was delighted. She didn't "kowtow" once. And she didn't lie. She wasn't covering up what was true for her in order to appease him. Nor did she put herself down. Not once did she say she was sorry, for instance, or invalidate what she had done before. She also didn't put herself in a situation where she had to "stick to her guns".

Instead, she operated completely without artillery. She was in a new world, the world of direct appetite. She wasn't fixing the bad; she was going for the good. A few more wins (and requests), and Mark was complimenting her with what is probably the highest praise a man can ever muster for a woman (brace yourself): "You're being so reasonable."

How's that for a scream? Reasonable my foot. Within ten minutes, she was getting more devoted sex out of him than she'd had in a year. He'd been flipped into ecstasy, was responding to her like no tomorrow, and she was being "reasonable". I suppose that men don't need to know what's going on. They'll still be happy, turned-on and validated. And they will be in love.

Carol was also able to remember to close the cycle each time. After sex, she caught her old anger coming up, but instead thanked and complimented him. Mark was winning enough by now that he let himself enjoy some time with Carol afterwards, lolling about, instead of running away from her disappointment. He then confessed how much he missed their intimacy, too — that it wasn't only her.

Beautiful story? Similar stories are available year-round. You never need worry about your man dumping you. He'll be winning with you, and you'll be getting what you want. To get what you want from your man, find him right honestly for something, give him a problem he can solve, then give him a win when he solves it.

Rowing to Australia

It's critical to remember this last stage. He's just produced for you, after all. Give him a win for it. Let him know he did well.

Luckily, it's a little easier at this point to find him right, because your appetite and person have just been satisfied. But what if Mark were not the best lover in the world, or Carol's experience wasn't the best she'd ever had? Maybe it was even disappointing. If you end up in a similar situation, whatever you do, don't give in to castration. Don't trash all the progress you've made so far.

When a baby is just starting to walk, do you punish him if he falls down so he'll know that falling is wrong? We hope not. We hope you encourage your child at every step. Train your man the same way. You're the power. Keep your self-esteem and stay away from criticism. Castrate him now, after he thought he was doing well, and it will be a long time before he comes around again. All the time, he'll be hurt, closed down and definitely no fun.

Keep going for the good. If you want your man to row you to Australia, break the task into problems he can solve:

"Honey, you're so much fun to be with. Let's go to the beach." (Which you two do.) "This is great — thank you for taking me. I love you being romantic. Let's take a walk along the water." (You do it) "Yeah! You're the best … You are so strong. Can you row me around a little?" (He does it.) "You are good at this. You are a wonderful boatman. Can you row out to that buoy over there?" (He does it.) "You're incredible. I am really impressed that you got us out here so far. Can you row double this distance from the beach?"

And so forth, until you sight the Australian shore. Find him right, break the big desire into solvable pieces, and keep expressing what you want. Praise him when he produces. You'll find yourself discovering new freedom and mastery, and all the while he will be a winning and accomplished man.

Maureen: *Team spirit*

The power of women's appetite was revealed to me during one of the worst times in my life. I was at odds with my estranged husband, living in our home with four teenagers, struggling to make ends meet with $100 a week and feeling neurotic. Then my 13-year-old girl, Lara, insisted on hanging out with her older sisters of 17 and 18. This would have been okay, but the boys they associated with were black-leathered, motorcycle-riding, mohawk-hair styled hoodlums.

Then Lara started coming home defiantly at three and four in the morning when she wasn't even supposed to have gone out. I completely ran out of patience one of these mornings and decided to send her to a New Zealand boarding school for girls. Her father and I were not on good terms, but he agreed to help if I could get her into a good school.

The process, however, was hell: schedules, air fare, transcripts and calling 40 separate schools, all full due to school having started. And then a stroke of luck. One of the more exclusive schools had one bed available, and the headmistress agreed to interview me, even though I was not a dignitary or diplomat. I flew 640 km south and did the best I could to make Lara sound like a good student.

Somehow, dazzling and baffling this headmistress, I got her in. Registration and uniforms required $5000. With relief, I called her father on the phone that evening, and was promptly informed that he "didn't have the money". He had it, of course. Another appetite had intervened while I was gone. Lara had convinced him not to pay. I was devastated. I went to the bedroom and slept for three days.

In the meantime, mother was taking my phone calls and making my excuses. As it happened, one of my callers was an elderly gentleman with whom I had lunched regarding an import business. At the time he was taken with me and so had called continuously for two days. At some point, my mother sensed he might be able to help, so she relayed my circumstances to him. Her intuitions were right. He said, "Why don't you both come to lunch with me? I think I can help."

We all ended up at the fanciest place in town: classical music, delicious food and the best champagne. Though it was a tough role to play, I did my best to be gracious. After lunch, he said he needed to speak with me alone. "I hardly know you," he began, "and I don't ever want to hear about this again.

I don't need to be thanked. I don't want anything for it. I just need to do this." He then handed me a cheque for $5000.

He then told me a story about his wife, now passed away one year. She disapproved of him once for not giving money to a door-to-door collector for a charity. She herself had rushed out after the person and given the donation. It was the one thing he still had to do for her.

I must admit, this was the most dramatic, intense and miraculous sequence of events I have ever been part of. But when my own appetite wasn't strong enough to counter that of my own daughter, I was able to get what I needed from a virtual stranger who wanted nothing more than to respond to the appetites of three powerful women — myself, my mother and his own wife.

So there sit the men at the bar. They are their own men, with their "freedom", not having to answer to anybody. And when one of them gets up and leaves because he promised his wife he'd be home early, every one of them wishes they had a woman who was using them. Men won't say this, of course. And in fairness, some may shudder at the memory of past castration. But every man at the bar wants to win with a woman. Every man wants a woman to use him and be satisfied by him.

Letting it float

We need to mention something important. You do not have to play nursemaid to your man. When we say give him wins, that's all you have to do. You find him right, you give him a problem he can solve for you, and you give him a win when he produces for you. That's it. You don't have to figure out how to do it for him, or worry about how he's progressing, or worry *if* he is doing it, or hover over him. Just relax and float. Enjoy the process.

When a woman tells her man that he is capable of doing something, he absolutely believes he can. If you're clear you want something, all you have to do is give him praise, and he'll produce. It's how he is put together. Powerful women know it.

123

Your want list

You are going to start getting powerful right now. You should have a list of your wants in front of you. Every woman should have a want list. From minor wants to major wants, you need to make up a list of everything you could possibly desire. But before you pin them above the kitchen sink, or above your bed, you need to talk to your man a little. He could freak out, you know.

So let him know that you have an assignment for him. Since you just want to enjoy having your desires expressed, his job is to enjoy it as well and to enjoy the process — no matter how long it takes — of getting them. He may also enjoy producing them from time to time, but if he doesn't completely enjoy this *process*, you will tear up the whole list and never again tell him what you want.

Maureen: *Down in black and white*

When I first heard about this want list idea, I swear it was as if God had spoken. I rushed home, pulled out a piece of paper and went crazy. I was really ballsy. I wanted a new gold ring with three diamonds — artfully arranged, similar to my friend, Beth's, but with rounder edges. I wanted a two-week Mediterranean cruise, then a month in Greece. I wanted a great gown I had just seen. I wanted financial independence and I wanted to be more in demand as a speaker.

Then I stopped short. It was like water splashed in my face. The next part of the assignment was to post it in the bedroom, and I started thinking how Geoffrey would react. He was either going to hit the roof, go into shock, or both. "Okay, fine. I don't have to post it anywhere. I don't have to show anyone. This is too much fun to stop. Besides, this is all honest for me. I'm not lying."

I said good riddance to my guilt and stayed with the programme. I wanted a new computer. I wanted land. And then I noticed something happening. Once I had listed all the biggies,

I found myself wanting simpler things. I wanted the fence fixed where the dog kept getting out. I wanted a bubble bath. I wanted two hours by myself each day. I wanted the latest novel by a favourite author. I wanted a heel repaired. I wanted champagne on the beach at sunset every once in a while. I wanted to sing songs. I wanted Geoffrey to make dinner. I wanted a neck rub.

I tell you, this is the best thing you can do for yourself. Sit down and write exactly what you want. Big or small, expensive or cheap, complex or simple. Write down the truth for you. What do you want? Include it all. That way, your man can respond at any level, and it is always a win. By the way, I did let Geoffrey see it. I titled it "Maureen's Important Wants", put it in an envelope and laid it on his dresser. Below in parentheses was, "At least you can't say you're with someone who doesn't know what she wants."

His reaction? Pretty good, actually. He was a little unbelieving at first, though he had a sense of humour about it. But the next day he surprised me and said, "I am so excited about your birthday list" (his idea is that any day can be my birthday). He claims he has had a lot of fun getting me things. Most are the little items. But a couple have been biggies. So, naturally, I keep adding things as I think of them!

When both of you are enjoying this process, you will be amazed that what you want will keep turning up magically. Maureen received her ring (above) about six months after she wrote it down. Her sister had been given a ring four years before, but had never got it fitted. She sent it to Maureen as a birthday gift, and it was the exact description on the want list. Maureen asked her how she knew, but sister didn't have a clue. Friends of ours describe it like this: "When we are making-out great (having a great time, and having great sex), people come in and throw money on the bed." When you enjoy yourself having your wants, when you enjoy the process of getting them, and when you let go of the struggle to get them, desires get fulfilled naturally. This isn't fantasy; this isn't voodoo; this is pleasure and power.

Chapter 11

The African Queen
*Where you understand the heroism of femininity
and the powerful role of dialogue*

We use a magnificent word, a magnificent concept, to talk about successful man-woman relationships. The word is "dialogue". We know this word may sound a bit scholarly at first, but it's the only word that works. Your authors are going to use it in a new, exciting and very precise way. For starters, we mean it as the exact opposite of *monologue.*

A monologue, you may know, is just one person talking. When you were a teenager, and a parent sat you down and solemnly lectured you, that was a monologue. That was one side laying down the law, or one side convinced they had the right answer. You can always spot a monologue, because the listening side is squirming. At the least, a monologue is dull and deadening. It has no sense of interaction or discovery. At the worst, you are being closed in, silenced, or in some relationships even injured.

If you did everything your man told you to do, for instance, that would be nothing but a monologue, and it would be a dying relationship. Or if he did everything you told him to do, that would also be a dead monologue. Both of these are just examples of oppression, and they aren't any fun at all. In fact, this is why some women feel shy about "running" or "using" their men. The idea of their powerful appetite running the whole show sounds like such a monologue, as if they're going to become domineering puppeteers pulling every string.

But relax. You are much more graceful and classy than that,

and you know it. That appetite of yours loves to play. It loves the interaction, the game, the give and take. It loves dialogue. As you read this book, for instance, you are engaged in a dialogue of sorts. You are *interacting* freely. You are speaking this book to yourself and gauging your responses. It seems that the best parts of human life are all about this kind of creative interaction, this sense of open participation and discovery.

At the same time, true dialogue is this experience of freedom as it occurs against the backdrop of your appetite or purpose. So your dialogue with your man will always be moving forward to what you want, yet it will not squelch him. It will engage him. You certainly want things from your man, but you also want him producing it out of his own excitement and freedom. Dialogue is therefore much more earnest than, say, a pleasant conversation, which has no real direction. A pleasant conversation is fine, but dialogue is different. We're talking about having your man's full attention on you during the resistance and attraction he goes through to become excited about what you want.

Dialogue is both the power *and* the play, both serious *and* fun. Your man is getting hitched up to your desires, but you are hitching him up in such a way that he feels free.

So don't worry about your man agreeing with you! He may agree with you at some point, but the point of agreement is actually the end of the dialogue. In a dialogue, things are a little unbalanced, but they're moving. The outcome is uncertain, but the game is in play. Dialogue actually lives in the interaction between differences. And this is why it is the sum and substance of every great romance you've ever known — whether in fiction, or in life.

So far, this discussion might seem a little abstract. So let's get specific: remember *The African Queen?* It turns out that this classic movie has just about everything in it you'll ever need to know about dialogue, heroism and romance. The reason it is so many people's favourite movie of all time is because it resonates naturally with their innate sense of romantic interchange and play.

Advanced sex education

The movie starts out with a shot of Humphrey Bogart, "Mr Alnut", in a man's idea of heaven: a native is dropping grapes in Alnut's mouth as he obliviously steams along an African river (in his boat named the same as the movie title). Alnut is perfectly happy. He has his little life in a boat, with his servant and his mail-delivery job. If a man has any appetite at all, this is about the limit of it. But it seems that "Rose" (Katherine Hepburn) will have other plans for Alnut.

It won't be just romance, however. Germans come and destroy the mission village where Rose lives, forcing her to escape with Alnut on *The African Queen*. She then finds out that the Germans have a battleship strategically located on a lake miles away. Alnut's plan is to lay low, but Rose wants justice. She wants to destroy the battleship. Her personal agenda is cloaked in patriotism, but underneath is a driven woman, a woman with appetite.

Infinite force meets unshakable obstacle

Alnut now starts to undergo the bends as he rises up from under 20 fathoms of unconsciousness. This outlandish woman is convincing herself with alarming speed of their duty to achieve the impossible. Armed with her first-hand experience of German cold-heartedness, her desires are lurching out and scaring the pants off Mr Alnut.

Remember his response? The love-coo of the human male? "Lady, you're *crazy*!" First, nobody has ever braved this river; second, there are no maps of it; third, the part they do know has deadly white-water runs; fourth, even if they could make it past the rapids, a German fort perched on the bank will sink them; fifth, even if they make it beyond that, there are miles and miles of feverish swamp to negotiate; and sixth, the two of them have no way to take on a fully manned battleship with his little steamer.

This is best characterised as the *nuclear fusion point* of man-woman — an infinite force meets an unshakable obstacle.

Woman's powerful appetite meets man's reasonable resistance. So does Rose give in? It would be a short movie if she did. What is brilliant here is how she maintains her appetite and reconfigures it according to the facts held up by Alnut. She doesn't criticise Alnut, nor does she ignore him. She does the most powerful thing she could do: she begins a dialogue. She continues expressing her appetite as it *interacts* with his point of view. Alnut knows the reality out there, after all. He has useful information. She, on the other hand, knows the truth of her vision. The challenge is to enter into dialogue to integrate that vision into a functional plan.

Dialogue of possibility

You see, most men would say that it's all a functional world. Things happen in a linear sequence. Cause, effect and logic. Sure, logic can serve as a good "reality check", but it takes up only a couple of your channels. You still have ten other cylinders firing, so you can derive new possibilities out of old material. Logic serves your appetite, not the reverse.

So Rose considers Alnut's resistance, then answers back with new possibilities at every turn. Alnut: "No one has even been down that river until recently." Rose: "Yes, Spencer was his name, wasn't it? If he can do it, we certainly can." And most importantly, she remembers to feed the machine: "I have every faith in your ability, Mr Alnut." Rose is wholly unreasonable. But that's what makes this movie, and life, heroic. "Reasonable" follows from what is presently the case; "unreasonable" creates a whole new world.

Until this chapter, we have recommended you simply train your man as you would a show dog, but that beyond this, he's as stupid as wood. This has been useful, because many women need to find out that they are the ones in the driving seat. But true mastery involves dialogue. Dialogue is the birth of freedom, choice, creativity, involvement, thinking on your feet, and all the great stuff about human life. It is where the juice in life is.

Dialogue is the basis of your relationship. You can use and trust this process of dialogue, because men, luckily, are accurate responders. Trust their responses, but still keep expressing yourself in the light of those responses. You can allow both. Listening is not losing. Allow the give and take of dialogue, and continue to express your appetite, or everything will fizzle into dead, tyrannical monologue.

The fountainhead of civilisation

This discussion goes beyond your relationship. Womanhood is the fire of human evolution. We have seen how feminine appetite encounters the resistance which is natural to male production and functionality. Within this nuclear fusion point of appetite, resistance and reconciliation, the very medium of human dialogue, *language*, was birthed.

Anthropologists once proposed that "hunting men" gave rise to language (discounted — hunter-men don't talk much … ever notice?) Then they proposed that playing children generated language, and recently they have proposed that "gossiping women" gave rise to human language. It has taken a while to get around to women (big surprise), and even so it's centred around what men consider the most trivial of feminine activities. But it's time to point out the obvious again.

Not women's gossip, but women's *power*. Women's appetite. In general, there are four things that separate humans from animals: 1) the sophistication of our language; 2) our level of productivity and civilisation; 3) the fact that women are the only females who experience orgasm; and 4) the fact that women are not limited in sexual readiness, but are continually calling their males.

Desmond Morris said it on page one of his introduction to *The Naked Ape*. Humans differ from other primates in two ways: larger brains and larger genitals. Our species is wrought in the push and pull of sexual dialogue. Your large lips and breasts, your pronounced curves, your abundant scent — and both sexes' hairless skin, armpit odour, even ear lobes — have little purpose, apparently, other than to communicate sexually.

Even our faces grimace and express sexual and emotional states like no other species. Now figure in 1) a tremendously longer sexual courtship than any other primate; 2) a much longer period of actual coitus; and 3) the fact that women are the only female primates orgasmically motivated. It is no mystery why the sexiest of the primates turns out to be the smartest, most communicative and most civilised.

Language didn't give rise to sexual dialogue, but the opposite. Evolution is not driven by signs and symbols, but by sexuality and reproduction. Anthropologists have been puzzled by why our brain's language centres do not seem to have emerged from those areas responsible for maths, reasoning, spatial relations and abstraction. It is because the heart of language is not abstraction — it is desire and response. Our language centres evolved directly out of the hypothalamus, the brain centre for smell, deeply felt emotions and sexuality.

But don't stop with language. Women have also directly fuelled our high level of production — that is, civilisation. Women's intense and sustained sexuality not only brings men into dialogue with appetite, it simultaneously enrols them to produce for it. Remember — unlike any other primate, men are producing for this appetite 12 months out of the year! After we then consider *additional* appetites beyond sex — security, home, children, baubles, status — human civilisation becomes, not an anomaly, but an inevitability. Where appetite meets production, man-woman dialogue provokes language, community, progress and civilisation.

But of course, this explanation is unthinkable. It is neither male-oriented nor pain-oriented. Human civilisation from women? No! Even more disagreeable — civilisation specifically resulted from their abundant and prolonged sexual appetites? First recognise women, and then recognise sexual *pleasure*? It's too much! So anthropologists may consider our idea, or laugh at our idea, but you need only hold the information as a back-burner intuition.

Similarly, don't worry about doing this dialogue perfectly. The three steps of The Training Cycle will keep you in the game safely and productively. If you get confused, just remember that dialogue comes from your appetite. Express your wants, and dialogue will take care of itself.

Appetite makes the movie

That's what Rose does in the film. She just expresses her de-sires, and the man responds. At one point, Alnut had described how he hated his work back in America. He announces brightly, "Out here I'm my own boss." Then he looks at Rose and scowls: "Anyway, I was until ... ." He fails to finish the sentence. Rose's appetite is running the show whether Alnut likes it or not.

It throws him into full-blown production panic. So he does the elegant thing by getting drunk and refusing to continue. The next scene finds Rose dumping out his gin, one bottle at a time, with Alnut too hung-over to stop her. Instead of her previous series of wins, Rose now withdraws into reading the Bible, an instinctive reaction to outfox and control him.

The game without rules

The strategy works. In the very next scene, Alnut is shaving himself happily, shouting to Rose how great it is to "have a lady aboard with clean habits." When again there is no response, Alnut complains that her silence is unnatural. Her response: "Nature, Mr Alnut, is put in this world to rise above." Finally, he can't take it any more. He pleads, "Fair is fair, miss. Have a heart."

Of course, Rose isn't interested in "fair". Men are fair. "Fair" is for the world of men's games. But women are up to much bigger things — like getting what they want. So Rose finally deigns to tell him. Not his drunkenness, but his refusal to keep his word, has angered her. Alnut has received the equivalent of grace and so agrees to continue on. Her hero once again, it is little wonder that in the very next scene, the two make love.

Once this happens, all bets are off. Both have given up their resistance to each other. Rose's whole look has changed. From this time on, instead of appearing brittle and tense, she appears beautiful and graceful. And Alnut is so happy he doesn't know what hit him. A man with confidence and purpose. "Then you think we can do it?" Rose asks him.

Alnut replies, "Do it? Of course we can do it. Nothin' a man

132

can't do if he believes in himself."

Rose's answer? "Thank heavens for your strength."

A man who believes in himself is simply a man who is responding to his woman's appetite. The powerful thing about romance is that it happens to work effectively in that cold, hard, physical world out there. That's what appetite is all about — receiving real things in the real world.

The vulnerable option

So the fact that Charley has now become confident and Rose has doubts is not a case of submission to stronger, more intelligent man. Rather, she now simply allows herself to have her doubts and her vulnerability. Yet this may upset some women. Women who have been misunderstood or hurt by men would probably rather die than be vulnerable with a man again. But if there were somehow a way to end all that pain and grow in genuine trust and safety with a man, would you take it? Could you bring yourself to have that pleasure again?

We're not saying that being vulnerable and "feminine" is your only option. You will have more things going than you can guess. You might want feminine, then masculine, then neither, then sing a happy tune. If you want to work on cars, join the military, be a sexy bimbo, research cures for cancer, be a traditional housewife, kick butt in the corporate world, or do them all in succession, do it. Whatever it is you want, we would be fools not to support you in getting exactly that. Getting what you want is what this book is all about. What Rose's character discloses is that having your vulnerability discovered by a man does not necessarily mean you are a welcome mat to a reigning-class pig. There are ways to allow yourself this intense pleasure in an environment of natural trust with your man and natural validation for both of you. Your appetite, with the Training Cycle dialogue, lets your pleasure happen naturally.

It also produces for you under any circumstances. Again take inspiration from Rose. At one point, she and Alnut are plummeted down a terrifying waterfall which destroys *The African Queen*'s propeller and strands them in the middle of the jungle. But Rose is undaunted by this change from the miraculous to the grimly real. She again finds her man right and competent, suggests new possibilities and praises him at every step of progress. To fix the boat-machine, Rose first fixes the man-machine.

Dialogue of romance

But the real miracle is the interaction which ensues, probably the apex of beautiful, winning, romantic man-woman:

Alnut: Aren't you proud of yourself?

Rose: Certainly not — look at the way you kept the engine going. Look at how you mended the propeller. It wasn't me at all. I don't think there's another man alive who could have done it.

Alnut: Right you are, Rosie, cause there's no other man alive who's got you.

Before we leap in and brand such dialogue as corny, not to mention sexist and self-effacing for Rose, could we just take a moment and appreciate its sweetness and generosity? This is a winning man-woman relationship. Rose completely validates Alnut for his competence and production; Alnut completely validates Rose for her attractiveness and inspiration. Don't let your cynicism and your politics jump in too quickly here. Instead, hope that you have this joy at least once again before you die.

And, yes, we know — Rose does not have to negate her heroic role in all of it. She has simply lost interest in being the person having to cause it all. Everyone knows she's the hero, that she's the true African Queen. But she's far beyond us — right now, she would rather enjoy the heaven of her relationship.

It is heaven for both of them. The last thing Alnut does before Rose and he face execution together, is ask that they be married. Alnut's heroism finds all of its source in his woman, and in the love and power that she wields. The only bridge between "Lady, you're *crazy*" and "I do" is appetite.

Chapter 12

What About This Femininity?

Where you expand self-esteem by learning both the dynamics and pitfalls of your own appetite

Femininity. Power. Attraction. Appetite. Femininity seems to be everything at once — not exactly forceful, but powerful. Approving, but guiding to something different that is wanted. Generous with him, but constraining him. It is not surprising, therefore, that many feminists have viewed femininity as a sham — an impossible meeting point of schizophrenic male demands. "Men want whores, men want mothers." But this isn't the whole story. From time to time, maybe women want to be whores, and maybe women want to be mothers.

Yet we acknowledge that this thing called "feminine appetite" contains a fundamental contradiction: it is a contradiction between the two words. That is, we have described "appetite" as something which is supposedly powerful, whereas "femininity" has always been associated with being passive. So which way do you jump when we talk about your "feminine appetite"?

Given your education in male society, of course, few of you will demand an explanation of why "powerful" is a good thing. So the word that probably worries you is "passive". To understand feminine appetite, we should look at this passive understanding of femininity. Is there anything redeeming about passive behaviour? What is it that could ever be attractive about playing a "passive" role? Why do some gay men, for instance, prefer such a personality and lifestyle?

One idea that people have put forward is that it is a way to avoid responsibility in a throwback to dependent childhood. If so, it might manifest as childish manipulation — a constant desire to be rescued, or possibly as a state of unhappy victimhood. Some women do seem to fall into these categories, so such a notion of femininity carries weight. But isn't this "childhood" option the same thing as being a little girl? It seems more of a pitfall than a definition.

Unlike the world of the child, then, feminine appetite is also sexual and powerful. Could this be it? Is it a means to gain power by using sex? Some argue this: women are forced to use sex to get the power that has been denied them. Again, we agree to some extent. Submission socially is sometimes domination sexually. But we're still missing something.

The anatomy of pleasure

As with most ideas conceived in this society, the role of pleasure is appallingly under-represented. Even some of our own readers may still be reluctant to consider human pleasure as having any real significance. After all, it doesn't manufacture anything. Pleasure is nothing but self-indulgence, isn't it? Many people will try to convince you of that. But we believe that pleasure, that inner motivation of appetite, is the founder of civilisation. And here is the difficulty — pleasure does not appear to be "productive" so much as it appears to be "receptive". It's another reason why the people of a producer-society would declare it to be useless or decadent.

But pleasure has it both ways. Pleasure embodies the same contradiction we find in the phrase, "labour of love". Love, of itself, is something enjoyed, something essentially passive. Love is pure pleasure. But labour comes of it. Production comes of it. A labour of love is just pleasure. It's not self-indulgent; it's more like self-indulgent *and powerful*. The contradiction permeating femininity and appetite is the same. So let's look at that aspect of pleasure which is the "passive receiver" instead of the producer — that aspect which is an effect instead of a cause.

James: *Intensity at effect*

If I am sitting in my living room, passively gazing out of the window, and my wife sneaks up behind me, slyly reaches around and slaps my face, the pain is much more intense than if I had seen it coming. If I cannot anticipate the slap, I am completely at the *effect* of it, and the pain is more intense. Fortunately, the same principle holds with pleasure. If I have a sore neck, and I reach back to rub it, it will certainly feel better, but it will be about one-quarter as pleasurable as if someone else rubs it for me.

Wouldn't we all like someone to come around each workday and give us a 20-minute neck rub? That is, wouldn't we love to be able to function, not as the *cause* this time, but as the effect? When I cause my own experience, my pleasure becomes diluted. But when I can relax and receive the massage, the pleasure increases about four times. For sex, make it twelve times.

So we need to become comfortable with a couple of terms here — "at cause" and "at effect". These two terms are central to the dynamics of pleasure. Simply, "at cause" means "in control". A person who is at cause is making things happen, consciously directing events, anticipating the fruits of his or her actions. But a person who is at effect is enjoying the ride. This person has pulled back from the direct role of making things happen. He or she is now emphasising the part of life that is experienced, instead of the part that is acted out or achieved. Of course, these two poles change. At different times, we all want to "stop and smell the roses" and experience the pleasure in life. But then we also want to get into gardening those roses — the sense of accomplishment.

So being at effect does not necessarily imply traditional feminine passivity. It can be traditional, but "at effect" really just means receiving pleasure. Being placed at effect — letting go of control — is where pleasure is allowed and intensified. It is nothing more nor less than being swept off your feet.

Needless to say, being "swept off your feet" did not originate with our book. It has been the dynamic of man-woman relationships since forever. It is actually the equivalent of romance. Women in long-term relationships state that, more than anything else, they desire to be swept off their feet again. It is not the product of male hyper-dominance this time, but of women's appetites.

Rape

We have said that women call, and men respond. We have said that women's appetite for romance is the appetite to be swept off their feet — put at the effect of a man. And then we say that pleasure, of all things, is heightened when a woman feels so at effect and out of control. Is this an invitation to rape?

No. Terms are being confused here. A rape victim is *not* pleasurably at effect — this is obvious. A rape victim is still actively resisting on one or more levels — physical, emotional, mental. This victim has not chosen to be placed at effect within an environment of trust and safety. Being pleasurably at effect means feeling safe enough to choose that intense experience, safe enough to choose consciously to let go of control. Any man who rapes a woman deserves the full penalty of the law.

Maureen: *Rape and law*

But what about women's fantasies of rape? A close friend of mine was actually raped at knife-point by a man who forced his way through her front door after watching her wheel her two-year old along the sidewalk. He was eventually caught. At the trial, she was asked, "Have you at any time fantasised about being raped?"

She thought for a moment, decided to be truthful, and said, "Yes." On that basis, she lost the case.

Our male-dominated legal system equates a sexual call with finding a woman *willing* to engage in sex. The two are completely different — the win/lose machinery of men cannot understand the sophisticated interplay of women's calling. The very thing that makes men easy fish to snag makes them grossly stupid and violent when they encounter losing and rejection. Even after our panda lopes 13 kilometers, the female still has the option to reject him. This is the game. Women call; they also reject. A man only needs to pay the bare minimum of attention to his woman, only as much as a panda does.

We're convinced that rape happens when a man thinks he is the one who originates sexual turn-on. This way, his ability to interpret his responses to women is completely obliterated. Instead of responding to a woman, a rapist is responding only to a desperate fantasy running in his head. He is cut off from the whole process of life and pleasure. Instead of the mutual discovery and dialogue which a woman can initiate, rape becomes pure monologue, pure tyranny, pure sub-human ugliness.

A rapist therefore doesn't even have the potential to be used by a woman. He doesn't possess the possibility of becoming a man. Sex and pleasure is trampled underfoot in violence, much like women have been trampled underfoot in our pain-oriented culture. When no one is tuned in to the natural process of human sexuality — when pain, blame and control comprise the orientation of our world — we wouldn't know pleasure if it jumped up and bit us on the nose.

Pornography

If we had a beef with pornography, this would probably be it: that there's no training happening. There's no interaction, no ability to respond to a human being. There is no dialogue. There is certainly a sexual, visual "call" of women pictured in pornography, but nothing else is going on. We don't feel this flagrant sexual call is wrong; it's just that other natural, humanising pleasures aren't being explored. Like rape, it's pretty much a monologue. Of course, you and your man viewing pornography together solves most of the problem.

Seeing pictures of women in sexual poses seems to excite both men and women. Even women who report disgust looking at pornography also often report intense sexual stimulation

139

afterwards. So sharing such pictures with your man can be exciting for both of you, because you can indicate what does and does not turn you on. But if you don't want to, then don't. If it's not a pleasure, then it isn't.

Nonetheless, bad management has led to a lot of monologue out there. Attractive women often get labelled as "stuck up" simply because they are tired of being approached without regard to whether they are actually calling or not. The men involved blindly push on in the face of obvious responses to the contrary, thinking that if they just add more energy and intensity, they will be winners, not losers. Their emotional world is either score or lose, but in the sophisticated dialogue of sexuality, win/lose is pure stupidity. Men need to be trained in dialogue, trained that they are winners only when they respond accurately to a woman.

Environment of trust

So yes, studies show that a primary focus of many women's sexual fantasies is some variety of being overpowered. It's only natural. The reason for such fantasies is the same reason for wanting to be swept off one's feet: being overpowered and without control is that intensification of pleasure which results from being placed at effect.

Of course, as one might expect, the standard psychological explanation for conquest fantasies is pain-oriented. Psychologists say that women have been taught to view sexual feelings as so dirty and bad that conquest fantasies allow them to feel guilt-free for enjoying themselves. But this whole guilt explanation is overwrought, as well as inaccurate.

If fixing the guilt were important, once women became more comfortable with sex over many encounters, they would start to lose such fantasies. But recent studies indicate that the more sexual experiences women have, the *more* likely do they fantasise about being overpowered. Being overpowered is not fixing guilt, fixing the bad. It is positive pleasure. Fantasising about being at effect sexually is just the emergence of an appetite growing naturally toward more and more pleasure.

140

Paying attention

There is a scene in another movie, *Henry and June*, where, at a Bacchanal of some sort, a masked man grabs the character of Anais Nin and rapes her. He then removes his mask to reveal he is her husband. Though it was a fairly intense scene, a woman we were with claimed she liked it. The placing of the woman so at effect, yet safe all the time, was an attractive combination for her. When you experience the safety which comes with knowing that your man's total attention is on you and only you, then being at effect is a great source of pleasure.

Therefore, if you the reader happen to be a man, you get to put your woman at effect — say, act out a conquest scenario with her — only if she has first expressed her appetite for it. When you have provided an environment of trust and safety, she might be interested, she might not. In either case, you pay attention to her, not to you. If you continue ahead without her appetite for it, you are selling every real man down the river.

Aggression and pleasure

Of course, being at effect is not your only option for pleasure. Some women prefer a more aggressive, in-control role. Many women report they like to be on the top during intercourse, for instance, because of the feeling of power that it gives them. Other women have stated that they enjoy fellatio for a similar feeling of control over their man's experience. As mentioned, females of thousands of species are, and must be, the sexual aggressors.

Nevertheless, know that you will be considered wrong by some people if you want to be sexually aggressive, then considered wrong by others if you want to be placed at effect. Welcome to our world. It is only in this pain-oriented society that you have learned to doubt all your pleasurable instincts. It is in these sexless 90s, when custody suits have replaced sensuality, that you will be alone in discovering the dimensions of your personal pleasure.

In truth, your appetite will probably take you all over the

sexual spectrum: sexually aggressive, sexually receptive, both, alternating, whatever. It's all just the dance of your pleasure. Actually, many women find that as they become more confident in their womanhood, they are able to receive such pleasure while simultaneously guiding their men to produce it for them. This is just 12-channel awareness operating. You can remain conscious of your sexual call while still being taken on an at-effect ride. You can be "swept off your feet, in control".

Descent into victim

Until then, however, you may forget that you are the one calling the shots. The power, the confidence, goes out the window; the "at-effect" stays, and you sit there in fear, helplessness and anger. This dovetails directly into society's placement of you as second-class. From the effect position, you lose touch with your power. Suddenly, you are tied to the tracks waiting for someone to rescue you. You become a victim.

This sense of helplessness can also occur when your appetite shifts to different areas. You may have been in great shape when what you wanted was a lot of sex, but now you find yourself thinking about family, and you don't think you have any power to get your man to support that. Or maybe you are successful in your career and feel great about it, but you feel abandoned sexually.

Appetite changes all the time. But your power doesn't. Keep yourself on your toes and get what you want. Nothing is as unattractive as a powerful goddess playing victim. Can you imagine a big lumberjack-type fellow sitting in the corner, snivelling because he won't lift a coffee table off his leg? It makes you want to kick him in the pants to get him moving. Same thing with you. Turn it around — start calling, giving wins, and getting what you want.

Maureen: *Turning up the dials*

For me, femininity is not a *means* to power so much as it is power itself. Who I am is this feminine power. I can turn it down to zero, or I can turn it up to 12 on the Richter scale. About a year ago, I had a chance to take part in a modern-day Cinderella story. I had a date with a man named Spencer, a suave and charming hotel tycoon. We had met at a party and had stayed in casual contact via Christmas cards and such. Then he heard I was in town at one point and invited me to dinner.

It was probably the most exciting date I've ever had. It was like watching the movies, only this time I was in it. Yet I knew Spencer's life was replete with beautiful women, even movie stars, so the chance of developing an ongoing relationship with him from afar was meagre. Instead, I simply decided to enjoy my evening to the limit. What did I have to lose?

I was going to make an impact. I was going to project beauty, sensuality and femininity, and I was going to have my fairy-tale date with the handsome prince. Spencer apologised that this was the chauffeur's night off when he called for me in his Rolls Royce. (I would try to overlook it!) When he came inside, I was sparkling, and I could feel my presence flowing out from me to include everything around for miles. I remember saying to myself, "This is easy — I make myself happy from the inside out, from the depths of my soul to the whole world." As a result, the whole world reacted back the same way.

Upon arriving at an elegant restaurant, the waiter showed us to a special table. As we walked to it, my energy embraced the whole restaurant, yet at the same time I focused all my attention on Spencer. As a result, he was captivated with me, and the evening was even more romantic and marvellous than I could have envisioned. At one point when we were laughing together, the chef even walked up from the back to peek at us. And when we left the restaurant, all eyes were on us.

I was pleased when Spencer phoned me the next day to tell me that four different men had called him to ask who the new movie star in town was. Yet I only did what every woman can do: I turned up the dials to attract the attention I wanted.

Mothers and lovers

Though Maureen turned up the dials, she was *receiving* attention. At the very same time that appetite is being generated from within, it is also drawing attention from without. Such power in combination with being at effect is what makes this experience so fascinating and pleasurable.

This combination explains a vital feature of female sexuality. Academic types are fond of discussing the two images of women in literature which exist predominantly in men's minds: the mother and the whore, the nurturer and the seductress. But what most have overlooked is that women have the same fantasy. Women want a man who takes care of them, responds to them and produces for them. But from time to time they want a man who takes them over, turns them on and puts them at effect. They want mothers (good boys) and they want whores (bad boys).

These two coincide with the appetites we discussed before — food (mother) and sex (lover). The problem is that these can sometimes oppose each other. If your man is "lover", you are being placed at effect and swept off your feet. If he is "mother", *he* is at effect by being more obviously a direct responder to your wants. The transition between these two basic appetites can therefore create confusion.

Recognise, therefore, that your appetite is a complex and powerful thing that changes colours like a rainbow. You don't have to get stuck as a victim in any one colour. Just switch. Use The Training Cycle. When he is winning with you, believe us, he will take the initiative to sweep you off your feet again, or be a good "mother" again. But even when he is putting you at effect, the bottom line is that you are the one generating.

We're giving you options. We're letting you know that the domain of appetite, femininity, power and pleasure is as valid as the world of production and functionality. Even playing out a "little girl" role is valid — just so you know it and are getting what you want. Getting what you want is the acid test. But getting "stuck" in a role is the opposite of having options.

Maureen: *Becoming unstuck*

Some of us are "little girls", or "mothers", or "saviours", or "teachers", or whatever. We know who we are. Nothing wrong with any of these roles, but the danger is getting stuck in any one, because you will be severely limited in being able to get what you want. Not just from your man, but from the world. If you are stuck like this, the world will find you to be a boring victim.

One example is Moya, the eternal mother left to rear three young boys when her husband walked out. Moya still takes liberties dominating the lives of these 30 to 35-year olds as though they were children. To this day, she cannot comprehend why two of those boys can't stand being in her company.

I played "mother" a lot during my marriage — which was appropriate, of course — but I felt I was robbed of playing "little girl", which is how we started out. It turns out it was myself who robbed me. I had a notion that if I didn't play the part of super-mother, nothing would get accomplished. But then I started to resent my husband when he wanted me to play lover. I was too tired and exhausted to be able to switch roles.

As a result, he hankered after sexy women and never gave me the attention I craved — to be nurtured and treated like a little girl from time to time. After I saw the children through their teenage years, I decided I had experienced all the motherhood I ever needed. I still play the role once in a while, when my kids really want advice. But the rest of the time, I'm catching up on friend, lover, little girl, or whatever is the most fun.

So are you feeling stuck? Do you want the juice back, the romance back, and your man excited and productive? We have a lovely suggestion: get yourself sexually pleasured. Get yourself at effect, again. There is nothing which comes close to putting as much power, joy and juice in your relationship as getting enough sexual attention. The good news is that sex is a wonderfully *nuts-and-bolts* activity. You can always find your way back into the lap of grand romance with simple sexual activity. (So let's get cracking.)

Chapter 13

SexSexSexSexSexSexSex

Where you take a no-nonsense look at orgasm,
intercourse, foreplay, sexual teasing, tumescence
and sexual appetite

Any woman who thinks something is wrong with her because she fails to achieve orgasm during intercourse has been sadly misinformed. If you are a woman who does achieve orgasm during ordinary intercourse, that's great. It's just tougher to do than not.

Your sexual centre

How can we say this? Well, first, we have to establish what we're talking about here. If you do not know what or where on your body that lovely little 10,000-watt light-bulb, your clitoris, is, consult any anatomy book. What such a book may not discuss, however, is how this tiny clitoris is the centre of your sexuality.

Of course, a second "trigger point" for orgasm has gained some attention in the last few years — the Grafenberg or "G" spot. We talk about the G-spot later, because, if it renders any sensations at all, they are quite different from those of the supercharged clitoris. In truth, there are many areas in and around your genitals capable of nice, sexy sensations.

But the clitoris takes the cake. It has a higher concentration of nerve endings than anywhere else on your body. So when you want pleasure, on what do you think you should concentrate? Elbow or clitoris? The reason most women fail to have as glorious an experience of intercourse, the old in-and-out, as their men is simply due to the distance between the clitoris and the opening to the vagina.

146

But this doesn't seem quite right. Why so far away? Shouldn't women feel the same as men during intercourse? Shouldn't God have made it that way? Look, kids, God has thought it through way beyond you. Do you think God would put the organ containing the highest number of nerve endings right in the path of a baby five times the width of your vagina? It almost makes you think that maybe things are the way they're supposed to be.

Self-acceptance, self-perfection

Yet is there any way for us to encourage you to get more pleasure without making you feel guilty or inadequate? This is the crux of it. Guilt and inadequacy are so much a part of a pain-oriented culture. It used to be worse. Many women during Victorian times felt guilty for enjoying sex at all and visited doctors to be "cured". Most women today may know it's okay to enjoy sex, but they still feel intimidated to train their men to give them some. As a result, they may be anorgasmic. Or if a woman does achieve orgasm, she can always feel inadequate because she doesn't have multiple orgasms!

So first, the self-criticism has got to stop. Intercourse rarely generates orgasms for you simply because of the realities of the human body. And as for multiple orgasms, it turns out most women fail to have them. You may also have different experiences of orgasm at different times. Nor do you need to worry if your natural lubrication is not up to par. Who cares? Add a little of the commercial variety and keep going for your pleasure.

Some women even worry about what they look like or sound like during orgasm. But orgasm is where your turn-on is oriented in the first place. Whatever you happen to be doing during orgasm, we guarantee your man will think it is stunning. Simply put, there is never, ever anything wrong with you. Even if the last seven generations of your family were all angry Puritans, there were still millions of years before that of perfectly randy, turned-on ancestors who have carried forward their genetic propensities for pleasure right into the present. Right into you.

You have a solid legacy.

But what about that imperfect body of yours? Before making the first move to lovemaking, try stopping and looking at each other — admire that body over there. Find that body right and beautiful just as it is. At first, you might have some doubt and embarrassment, but it will soon add a dimension of mutual acceptance and admiration to your sexuality. The comparisons you regularly make between you and all those perfect bodies in magazines will start to fade away, and you will begin to discover that you are fine the way you are.

The holiness of sexuality

This discovery that there is nothing wrong with you is part of the holiness of sexuality. When your man is putting his full attention on your pleasure, he is allowing you to express your desires in the sanctity of being perfect. Putting full attention on another may be what love actually is. He is giving to you, and receiving from you, complete validation and consideration. What more could a human being ask for? Shouldn't we all be entitled to some of this treatment at least once in a lifetime? Yet 99.99 per cent of us receive none.

But you will. You're starting now. The place to start is with your own perfection, what you want right now, without the doubts, denials and criticisms that are so much a part of our lives today. If making love while hanging from a chandelier doesn't happen to give you the big thrill, that doesn't mean you're a dud. If your girlfriend tells you how her man dresses in scuba gear and uses the garden hose to bring her to an out-of-body climax, that's just fine.

Use that to interest and excite your own appetite if you want, but don't put yourself down. Smile and say, "I'm so happy for you!" This is your ball game only. The only standards here are yours. If you are in pleasure, you have won. You fulfilled your spiritual duty in life. We're interested in having you plumb the depths of *your* pleasure, finding out what *you* want, and then getting it.

PC means pleasure control

In this spirit, we have a little exercise for you. You already know that your authors are not crazy about work, but this exercise can be fun. Because so many women have had success with it, we have to include it. You've probably already heard about it. For years, doctors and specialists have known about the benefits of exercising a tiny muscle called the pubococcygeus, or "PC", muscle. Without this muscle, orgasm is virtually impossible, apparently. Other muscle contractions also accompany orgasm, but this one seems to be the most important. In fact, three out of four women who say they've never experienced orgasm turn out to have extremely dissipated, even wasted, PC muscles.

So where is it? Your PC muscle runs from the front tip of your pelvis to your tailbone and is the same muscle that contracts to stop the flow of urine. If you had your finger in the entrance of either your vagina or anus during an orgasm, you would feel it contracting a few times. The best way to identify it is simply to interrupt your own urination a couple of times. Afterwards, you can flex it any time you like: sitting, standing, walking, doing the dishes, singing on Broadway. Of course, it's a bit comical to sit around with your little secret, flexing away on your PC muscle during staff reports and PTA meetings. But why not? Pleasure is supposed to be about fun anyway. It's the absence of pleasure that is always so deadly serious.

If you happen not to be experiencing orgasm, it's probably a good idea to start such a programme. Counsellors often recommend about twenty minutes a day for two or three weeks. However, your condition could be anything, so consulting with a specialist is always important. Also, you should know that this exercise itself can be a turn-on, so you may need to be prepared for some tension of arousal, or for additional discharge of your lubricating fluid. A strong PC muscle is also a nice treat for your man, of course. The stronger it gets, the more you can control the pressure around his penis during intercourse.

Strengthening the PC muscle will strengthen anal sphincter

muscles somewhat, and this also intensifies orgasm. You don't need to be squeamish about the entrance to your anus being a source of sexual pleasure. Your anus may be second only to your clitoris in its concentration of nerve endings, so your man slightly inserting his finger here can be pleasurable, painful or both, depending on his gentleness and your preferences. In fact, an incredible way for both you and your partner to intensify orgasm is to push out on these muscles, the same as if you were having a bowel movement, right as your orgasm starts. You will be amazed by the deeply pleasurable sensation that results from simply pushing out.

A strong PC muscle will also improve bladder control, seeing as it is the muscle responsible. But remember that this exercise isn't just for women with a problem. You don't have to be in deprivation and pain in order to go for pleasure — remember? Even if you are currently having riotously wonderful, torrential orgasms, this exercise will heighten them. Of course, the main way to intensify your orgasms is to have one after another after another. But if you want to add a little pleasure fitness programme, this could be the ticket.

Hippopotamus gulps

We want to get you back in touch with that sexy appetite of yours. This world has left many of you out of touch with your sexuality. Bad information has left others without sexual satisfaction. Sometimes, if you hear about friends getting a lot of sexy attention, it may leave you with feelings of personal inadequacy or even envy. If so, don't worry. You happen to be right on target. Such envy is simply evidence of your appetite being aroused. You are not responding to sexual appetite in the head-over-heels fashion of men. You are the appetite itself. You are the sleeping tiger. And you are starting to awaken.

Since we are using zoo analogies, try this one out: imagine a huge hippopotamus with a dainty pink bib around its neck in preparation for a tastefully tiny meal. "Oh no," it says. "I couldn't have any of that food. Well — maybe. Only because you insist. I'll just have a tiny little nibble." The hippopotamus takes a

150

dainty bite, and in the next moment, half the table is down its stomach. This is women and sex.

It even describes a good girl like you. Still, sex is not *simple* for you. Women often do not allow sex to be as complex as it has to be for them. They have not learned to trust their own needs in this area, to take the time that their more complex sexuality requires.

Tumescence

There is a simple reason for this complexity — "tumescence". One of the most important things Mother never told you is the role of *sexual tumescence*. Some of you may be familiar with this term as it relates to a man's penis. If a man's penis is limp, it is "detumesced"; if erect, "tumesced", or swollen. The same thing occurs within the tissues of your vagina. When you are sexually aroused, you become swollen inside. Yet a different, very important part of tumescence is that dainty pink bib. Until you are in the process of being wooed, aroused and "sexed", tumescence manifests as the general sexual tension we discussed earlier — tension which is a *repelling* emotion.

As your cycle and hormone levels change throughout the month, tumescence comes and goes. But without any release, tumescence tends to show itself in physical and emotional pressure. You become tense, or sluggish, or easily irritated with people. We're sure you already know this. But what you may not know is that this tension is not necessarily a problem. Instead, it is a part of the swing and cycle of life, a necessary rhythm of your sex and appetite. All it takes to breeze through these times is to make sure you are having regular and frequent orgasms. How's that for a prescription?

Your man needs to know, however, that this resistance can continue right through your lovemaking, right until the eleventh hour of your orgasm. Some researchers claim that this is a natural instinct to fight and resist, ensuring that a woman has children by the best male. If he can make it past her smoke screen, he's the strongest male around. Whatever the reason, your man needs to be made aware of it. For instance, he may be doing just fine

151

touching and loving you, and all of a sudden you start thinking about new wallpaper. It can make him a little nuts if he doesn't know what's happening. In any case, with enough attention on you, you'll have no problems at all, because your body is being faithfully detumesced. Throughout Polynesia, for instance, it has widely been understood that the woman's orgasm should be sought deliberately to reconcile fighting between husband and wife. Orgasm has been seen as a way to release tension and restore harmony, reuniting the bonds of love and loyalty. Orgasm also does nice things like improving skin tone (by increasing oestrogen, researchers think), and alleviating insomnia, headaches, nervousness, even menstrual cramps.

So by now, you may be getting a better appreciation of how important those orgasms are. How important regular sex-ing is. However, we mentioned that it's also not this simple. Just on the physical level, sexual tumescence presents resistance to being touched. Once you are past that hump and involved in making love, the very same tumescence kicks in to fuel the fires. But generally, you have to start slowly.

Slow sex

You must have foreplay. We know this may sound trivial, but that's society talking. In a male, functional world, foreplay is equivalent to wasting time. "Why wait, when I'm turned-on now?" is the standard on/off point of view of most men. But sexual tumescence requires it. Your body requires it. Women generally have to approach the table with dainty bibs. The rest will take care of itself.

Researchers suggest that this "arousal period" allows time for the tissues and muscles in and around your pelvis to swell, and stretch tighter, as they engorge with edema fluids. These fluids are then expelled, in ecstasy, during the contractions of orgasm. Swollen tissues also reduce problems with painful insertion, because your vaginal opening naturally dilates as you are turned on. And as usual when you put your natural pleasure first, others get to share: tumesced vaginal tissues squeeze your man's penis more firmly and pleasurably during intercourse.

Admittedly, there is much less sexual sensitivity in these tissues than in, say, the shaft of a penis, another reason traditional intercourse is less exciting for you than for him. Even so, the famous G-spot is sometimes stimulated enough to give you a lighter orgasm. Other times, your clitoris pulls back into the moving folds of your labia and is stimulated second-hand. You can also experience a satisfying sexual fullness when penis or fingers push against these tissues. This is why a big penis, though fine, is not critical: the man who makes sure you are getting fully tumesced and swollen will create this sensation of fullness even if his penis is only a few centimetres long. Even this man can win with you. The nice thing about foreplay, however, is that it is defined as be*fore.* Before orgasm and release. If you are being tumesced, but you're not rising up toward the noble orgasm, you're sinking into pressure and stress. You are either headed toward orgasm, or you are headed towards resistance.

Sometimes, you're headed for both. You may be familiar with this experience if you ever have a hot date planned for the evening. In the morning, everything seems normal. But then let's say you receive flowers from your man, and you catch your breath just a little. As you think about the approaching evening, you drop something. An hour later, this fellow calls and says, "Remember — tonight is the night," and hangs up. Why did he hang up like such a jerk, you wonder, as you spill coffee on your dress. Brushing the coffee off, you break your fingernail. As evening approaches, you continue to feel lightly pressured. You feel more and more at-effect, surrounded, without a sense of control, and your tumescence increases.

Then he slides a card under your door with a picture of two lovers embracing. On the back he has written, "Thinking of you, my fiery lover — *Tonight.*" Now you are getting a little light-headed. You set the card down, and somehow manage to stub your toe and bump your head at the same time. You want to relax, but you can't figure out if you're coming or going. It turns out, you're both. Tumescence is building up on both sides of the coin. If he's ten minutes late, for instance, you'll want to strangle him. Until he gives you his own rapt embrace, at which time your knees will buckle with the pleasure of it.

It's all just tumescence. Once you get past the resistance, the ecstasy is yours. But this is the sticking point. It brings up an extremely important issue for men and women. Starting. Someone has to start. If day in and day out, nobody starts, you will be stuck with the most awful frustrations and anxieties you can imagine. So if he doesn't start, you'd better. It's survival.

One huge part of the resistance to starting is a whirlwind of mental claptrap and psychological debris that can attend on your tumescence like a swarm of gnats. It just never seems like the right time. You always have too much to do. Or you feel kind of sexy, but you don't just want to ask him for sex, like you would a beer. You don't even know if he's going to be interested. Or if you're going to be interested any more. You wish he would not just come up whenever he wants and grab you. Or maybe you wish he *would* grab you once in a while. It would almost feel better to have a good fight and sock him one — better than having to drop everything and instantly become receptive. Why does this feel so unnatural? What's wrong here? Maybe after we watch a little Tv ... and so on.

What can we say? Try not to get caught up in this garbage. It isn't worth it. Of course, if your mental racket is of the type that you still believe sex is dirty or selfish, you will never start. So instead of giving in to these taunts, whatever they are, just start. With enough sensual dedication, all of this mental trash piddles away into nothing.

Maureen: *Winning orgasms*

Dar's relationship with Jim was one of the best she ever had. He was a caring man with the same interests, a man she had fun with, a man who was nurturing to her. But she didn't have strong sexual feelings for him, and it worried her. It was similar to a case of "mother versus lover". But not quite, because *he* was always hot for her.

She would "give in" from time to time when she was tired and her resistance was down, but both were aware she was withholding herself. Then one morning, for some reason she let go. She just opened herself up to him. As a result, Jim became intensely focused on her — he was totally immersed in bringing her to orgasm. She also reported she hadn't climaxed so powerfully in two years.

But the pleasure didn't stop there. For a year, she had been complaining from time to time about being unable to get things done because she had to leave her computer at work. Later that morning, she mentioned it again. Jim stepped right up: "Don't worry — let's buy you a laptop. Put it on my card." Dar was amazed. *By letting herself receive from her man, she naturally acknowledged him.* As a result, he naturally provided for her.

Sweet surrender

Importantly, Dar was not faking a good time in order to trick her man into buying something for her. That would be no-pleasure, no-fun manipulation. Instead, this was honest and complete release of resistance.

The resistance of tumescence is a physical thing, but there is this psychological dimension to it as well. It is the realm of release and surrender. You don't need to torment yourself about it. As you begin to make more and more choices for pleasure, this resistance starts to fall away.

So the issue is again *starting* — getting past that tiny hurdle of tumescence which seems so big when you're on the no-fun side of it. Two things are required here: 1) a woman who is in touch with her own appetite, and 2) The Training Cycle. The way you start is with appetite, and the way he starts is with winning. Of course, if your man is already responding to you, wanting you, you don't have to worry so much about starting. You can resist him a little, then gradually get interested.

Accordingly, some day there may be a sequel to this book for men. It would have to do primarily with them paying attention to their women. But you know as well as we do, barely a tenth as many will read it. Men do not constitute the appetite for sex

155

and relationships. Fortunately, they are absolutely the appetite for winning. So a good man can actually be trained to watch the calendar and anticipate as much of your physical cycle as possible. Of course, you will have to tell him. Your tumescence will generally peak a week before menstruation, so this is a good time for him to start increasing his attention on you and his sex with you. Two weeks before menstruation is also good. Of course, most men already know this. Not.

Baffling orgasms

Not in this society. Sexual tumescence is considered to be a disease, "PMS". God forbid that anyone release tension with pleasure. That's backward. And silly. It's (snicker) not scientific. Plus there's no money in it. Researchers have tried hormones, surgery, tranquillisers, nutritional programmes, light therapy, even aromatherapy to "combat" PMS. But nobody receives grant money to investigate the therapeutic effects of pleasure. In a pain-oriented society, and a disease-oriented medical community, an abundance of sexual pleasure is way off the graph.

In fact, in the late sixties, a few scientists were interested in this area and started measuring the duration of women's orgasms. Most women in their group fell somewhere in a range from about three seconds up to maybe 40 seconds at the top. Except for one. One woman's orgasm lasted 17 *minutes*. What did they conclude? What any team of level-headed researchers would — she was a freak. So they eliminated her from the statistics. Of course, this woman did not feel like a freak. In fact, she felt great. It seems to us they should use her again, this time for PMS studies!

Since then, a few women have found they are able to sustain physically measurable orgasms lasting ten hours or more. This would certainly get out a few kinks, don't you think? These women practise at it, however. They practise expanding their capacity for pleasure. A fine book has been written about it entitled, *E S O; Extended Sexual Orgasm*. Check it out — how much pleasure can you handle, anyway?

But if sexual pleasure didn't seem over-emphasised before, it must by now. Orgasm for 10 hours? What's the point? What possible use could this have? The answer is that, thank God, it has no use. It does happen to be the source of civilisation, but you don't need to think about that. You don't need to wonder how it's going to manufacture bigger bridges and faster food. The only thing you need to worry about is which of these two statements you would like written on your tombstone: "She behaved herself"; or, "She let herself have passion, sensuality, romance and joy in her life."

You either get what you want, or you and your man can kiss it good-bye. You are an ultra-sophisticated, physical, cyclical, complex woman, the source of progress, sex and sensuality, and the harbinger of God-given appetite. Train your man to feed you. The Training Cycle not only allows you to express what you want, and not only fuels your man to produce for you, but it also lets you *fathom* more and more of your desire. So take your time. Have your man accommodate your natural tumescence by training him to move slowly. Enjoy the process of coming to orgasm. Take it in little intimate sections, little intimate discoveries. Or, when you prefer, in huge hippopotamus gulps!

The many roads to serenity

Earlier, we spoke of other ways to detumesce, not as effective as orgasm, but still good to know about. Most are physical. Someone giving you a big hug, for instance, or rubbing your shoulders — your whole body, for that matter. Even just the pressure of your man lying still for a moment on top of you. Or you taking a hot bath and experiencing silky creams and oils against your skin.

Less physical ways include things like conversation. A man can actually detumesce you just by putting enough attention on you to talk with you interestedly for a time. Another way is to receive all the classic forms of romantic attention such as flowers and cards. Of course, shopping is a winner. Each of these methods is nothing less than the first rung on the hierarchy

157

of your appetite: sex and all forms of attention to your person.

One other way you become detumesced may not be as much fun as these, but still somewhat effective — physical activity. "Spring cleaning", for instance, is apparently a response to rising sexual tumescence during the spring months. On the other hand, some kind of regular exercise — walking, dancing, whatever — is probably a good idea for releasing tension and aggression, and of course, improving health.

Digital sex

Before you run out and buy the exercise bike, however, try this: make sure your clitoris gets the attention it craves. Of course, different books demonstrate 100,000 or so different coital positions, some of which include the clitoris more in the act. But you know the best way to include it? Make it the sole object of attention. Since a penis doesn't quite do the trick, what possibly could? What could be coordinated and sensitive enough to interact with that tiny organ with the delicacy and subtlety required? His tongue? This is a good guess, but we have something else in mind. Something that hasn't been used to a fraction of its full potential. Fingers. Fingernails clipped short, please. And always make sure you use lubricant, just so long as it doesn't have alcohol in it which sometimes irritates tissues. Vaseline has been wrongly maligned, actually. Good old Vaseline is harmless to the body and has good staying power, which is nice at those critical moments when your attention is definitely elsewhere.

If you want, you can also mix in a scent you like. With Vaseline, you can melt it in a pan over low heat and add a scent that way. Then you can pour it into a more attractive container where it cools back into the Vaseline we all know. Whatever you choose, keep your lubricant near the bed, easily accessible. Also be sure to have a clean, dry towel accessible. Facial tissue generally fails to hold up, and ends up sticking to everything. Use a towel.

Also, since you are hopefully going to be spending more time loving and sex-ing each other, try to make sure both of you are comfortable throughout sex. No sacrificing here, no martyrs. This is about both of your pleasures, not about one of you doing "noble duty". He is lying on his side massaging your body, and his other arm is developing gangrene from no circulation? You don't want your pleasure at his expense. He thinks he's being gallant, but you don't need the favour.

Like all of us, he has been educated away from pleasure, so in lovemaking he can fall into the same goal-directed work behaviours that he uses in other areas of life. He always feels he has to give you an orgasm; or worse, he always feels he has to give himself an orgasm. But the rules of this game are different. It may seem like a subtle difference, but it means so much for both of you to pull out of goal-compulsions, and take a little time to pleasure yourselves.

So in this spirit, make sure you two have plenty of pillows, that you and he are able to ease up and change positions, that either of you can stop to urinate if need be, that your neck doesn't get slowly pushed into the headboard — common sense stuff. Common sense is usually the problem, however. "Common" is so tolerant of being in pain that it doesn't help much.

So your man can sit upright, cross-legged on the bed next to you, and use both hands in a labour of love to bring you slowly and heroically to orgasm. Or, if you like, quickly and heroically. Fingers of his second hand can be inside you while he massages your clitoris. Fingers at or in your anus is another area where nerve endings are highly concentrated and pleasurable. Or he can be lightly rubbing your breasts with his free hand. Or you may prefer he lie down next to you if his one free hand is enough. He can also sit between your legs facing you. Plus, of course, you can mix any of this, in any amount and any order, with any other lovemaking you like. But lubricated fingers are a great main dish. They also work nicely for you "doing" him.

Another benefit is that your man can learn to extend your orgasm. All he has to do the moment you are climaxing is drop the intensity of stimulation to between one-third and one-tenth of what it was. You let him know how much, of course.

159

Sometimes all it takes is the slightest "vibration" of his finger against and away from your clitoris. With this, a few women are able to double or triple the length of their orgasms right away.

Get yours first

So now that you're all spiffy and excited, we wish to introduce you to yet another radical concept in lovemaking. Or if you've already heard this we gladly re-introduce you — *get yours first.* Your man gets to attend to your orgasm first. We know that you all hold in your heart of hearts the golden dream that happens once every blue moon — having simultaneous orgasms during intercourse. And then both of you are breaking into song. But even if mutual orgasm happens more than once in a blue moon, it's rough to have it as a constant expectation.

For one, it's incredibly distracting. Two people having their attention on two orgasms, alternately wanting to get their own, but also wanting to be attentive to the other ... trying to achieve simultaneous orgasm is like two drunks standing in a hammock trying to hold each other up.

But when your man is doing you with his graceful fingers, two people's attentions are focused on one splendid orgasm. Your orgasm. You get yours first. It slows him down graciously, lets him win big with you, and in the meantime, you get just what the doctor ordered. Many women also report that when their men do them first, he attends to them more eagerly.

In any case, afterwards, and after you've enjoyed post-orgasm delirium, all kinds of possibilities open up. Your man has just produced for you big-time. He's your winning hero-lover. So you now have a chance to cuddle if you like. All it takes is a, "You were great, honey; hold me for a while." It's very pleasant to get some kind of detumescing action right after orgasm — being held, as mentioned, or your man rubbing your buttocks, shoulders, or legs.

Please me tease me

Now that you know where you're headed, we're going back to the most important part of all — getting there. We are proud to introduce you to the joys of being teased. Being teased is probably the most gratifying, extended opportunity for pure pleasure that you have. In fact, recent books on sexuality have gone into great detail about the sure-fire joys of being teased, gradually whipped up into an amorous frenzy.

Teasing is the highly tumescing, super-light stroking of your face, lips, hands, feet, neck, arms, legs, breasts, buns, nipples, clitoris, anus, etc. Using anything from feathers to fingers, your man can start with the most remote areas of your body — your hands, the underside of your arms, the backs of your legs — and gradually tease these locations with such light and delicious strokes that you soon guide him vigorously to more sexual areas. It takes time, it takes your man's full attention, and all the while your level of sexual excitement is building as if for a deluge.

It also allows you to establish a strong Training-Cycle dialogue with your man: he will be involved in a series of seductive wins and responses, so that when you do make love, the experience will be all-consuming. Orgasm is also usually intensified, because your physical sensitivity has been slowly enhanced while those orgasmic tissues of yours swell with sexual readiness. Being teased is one of the most loving and sensual experiences available to either sex, so you can also do it to your man. But that could be down the road a bit, as he is going to have less tolerance for it than you. Therefore, for starters, make sure you put serious time into getting some of this long-term teasing.

As teasing progresses, you and your man can discover all kinds of great techniques. A good one is for him to start with a wide circle around one of your breasts and then slowly, slowly spiral inward to the nipple. Right as he is about to touch it, he only lightly brushes it before he pulls his finger away. Then he moves to your other breast. Another one is for him lightly to stroke the upper backs of your legs, then start moving toward your buns. A little later, he moves slowly to the inside of your cheeks, and finally just lightly brushes the area around your anus.

From here, he can do similar moves in the area around your vagina, maybe touching only your pubic hair for a while and then slowly approaching and recoiling from the sensitive lips there. How quickly your man finally zeroes in on your clitoris and brings you to orgasm is, as always, up to you. You could be in the mood for a "quickie", or you may want the red carpet treatment we're describing. But you should know that as you get more in touch with your sexual appetite, being teased into ecstasy will become a very high priority.

Still, you have to give your man a clue how to bring you to such ecstasy. He is wired up only to do what he can win at. And he can only win at something he has received training in. Guess who will supply that training.

Chapter 14

Training Your Man in Sex

*Where you train your man sexually
and break unsatisfying habits*

You have to be willing to train your man if you're going to have
a good life, and if you're going to have good sex. It's the way
the species is built. The distance between vagina and clitoris is
the span of human training. You either tell him how to give
you orgasms, or you lose, he loses and your relationship operates at about three horsepower. Even if you're operating at 200
horsepower, and are quite-happy-thank-you, we're still not going
to let you off the hook.

Remember that prospect mentioned early in the book to go
for "better", even when you feel you already have it good? You
can try to hover in one place, but it won't work. Hovering is
what you do when you're not expressing your appetite. It is
also the state of uncertainty where your man is losing because
he can't figure out if he is winning or not. So we wish to
discourage you from trying to hover. We're here to remind you
to keep going for better. That's what the road to pleasure is all
about.

New tricks for old dogs

But without the structure of sexual training, the only thing left
for men is to interpret orgasm or not-orgasm as the only win or
lose options available. Remember that winning and losing are
not dry concepts for men. They are as intense and emotional as
love. In sex specifically, men's unconsummated turn-on is

equivalent to losing, so orgasm becomes the shining goal post of winning and validation. And here is where you can encounter a big problem. Once Mr On/Off is in the middle of winning with you sexually, he will go for the touchdown like a pig in heat. So the question becomes, "Who's going to get their parade rained on, here? My pleasure, or his win/lose ego?" But now, you both get to parade, because you have become a training master.

You easily employ The Training Cycle to deliver you from this dilemma by saying, "You are so hot! Could you slow down with me a little? Yes. Thanks, honey. That feels really good. I love that you are so intense. Could you take some time and massage my neck? Ahh. Perfect. That's great." Hopefully you're getting a better idea how this process works. The important thing is that he wins and you get what you want.

Winning and loving

You may notice, however, that we seem to have ignored his orgasm. Well, almost ignored it. There is a reason. He cares less about his orgasm than about winning with you. Does this sound too romantic to believe? Only because it challenges everything you have been taught. Women have been taught that it is their sacred duty to make sure he gets his orgasm no matter what.

There is nothing wrong with making sure he has an orgasm. He, for one, isn't going to argue with you. But we are saying clearly and emphatically that both men and women have been conned about this. He may not think it, but he definitely feels it. He wants to win with you more than he wants to ejaculate. Orgasm without winning validation is the booby prize. But when he is winning with you, that is when his experience of orgasm, when it does arrive, is deep, meaningful and incredibly pleasurable.

Maureen: *Spanish nights*

I was going through a man-hating stage. I had just broken off with a hopelessly ugly, entangled relationship. So I decided to take a break and accompany my Yugoslavian girlfriend, Jana, to Spain. We were very excited the first night we arrived, so we went out to a coffee bar for a bite to eat. Two extraordinarily handsome men soon walked in and smiled at us. Eager to flirt in this new culture, we smiled back.

The men responded immediately, came over and invited us out to a nightclub. We chanced it and accepted. Jana got in the front seat with Daniel, and I sat in the back with Luis. But before we had got far, without any warning, Luis reached over and pulled down the zipper to my pants. I was so shocked and violated, all my anger focused at once. I punched him so hard in the face that my ring drew blood. Luis was stunned.

I demanded that Daniel stop the car, and I opened the door to get out. Jana and I stepped out and started walking up the street in total darkness. But they continued to drive alongside, now apologising profusely and begging us to get back in the car. The upshot was that ... we gave in. I was now somehow confident that these men would behave themselves, but I knew I had to maintain the upper hand. So I became a complete bitch. I was incredibly demanding and, in fact, not once was I ever polite to Luis again.

This is all the more interesting since a couple days later we became lovers. When I finally decided to have sex with him, soon after I was finished, I ordered him to get out of my flat. In fact, every time we made love, I did that; it was great therapy for me. But not just me. Each time, Luis walked out ecstatic. He was a bigger man because he was responsible for giving me orgasms. He was winning with me, and he felt purposeful and masculine.

It wasn't really the sex for Luis — it was the winning. For Maureen, of course, it was the sex. But men are the lovers, and winning equals loving. Winning doesn't trivialise their love. But it does give us an appreciation of how close to home men's win/lose machinery is. He needs to win, and when he does, he falls in love. Of course, the primary win is your sexual satisfaction. Like Luis, a man who is giving you regular orgasms hardly needs to win at anything else.

Rape and the little Mrs

All we need to do to get to this level of winning and validation is to change a few painful habits from society. You are supposed to be a virgin, and he is supposed to be John Wayne. Virgins have no appetite, and John Waynes need no wins. Actually, John Waynes don't even need women. Just their horses. But guess again. Without wins and appetite, nothing ever happens. Without wins and appetite, you shrivel. Without wins and appetite, men have only one thing to do — get theirs.

Recently a woman came on Tv discussing being raped by her husband for the last 25 years. That is, he would get an inkling of turn-on, would roll over and start bumping around on her. She would usually ignore him or say she wasn't interested, he would mount her, have his orgasm, roll back over and go to sleep. Now *there* is an exciting love life!

Certainly she was calling him. She had a woman's body which gets as naturally tumesced and turned-on as any woman anywhere. Her husband was responding as men respond. But it doesn't justify anything. He leans over without saying a word, feels her resistance and continues anyway? That's rape. We can't think of a clearer definition. The only big question is whether their sex life could be considered mostly sad ... or mostly dismal.

Bad information

We have all been given bad information. You can always recognise it. It's where the misery is. For those of you trying to figure out who was the bigger loser above — the helpless handmaiden or her exciting husband — don't waste your time. They both were. The woman was so alienated from her sexual appetite that she disappeared off the face of the planet. After 25 years of that stuff, she loathed the very idea of sex because nobody had ever taken time with the poor darling. The fact that other women seemed so interested in sex never made sense to her. Or it was vaguely deflating.

On the other hand, her husband was a loser every time he was with her. This particular fact, of course, never crawled the entire distance up to his razor-sharp mind. Instead, it just slowly drained the life out of him. His sexual experience was as wonderful as slurping the dregs from an old barrel of wine. Pretty paltry, but if it's all you know, hey, it's great. And that is the point. If the information is bad, if it's all you know, you will never seek anything better. This story is about ignorance. It's a story about how far we've got away from the natural pleasures of living and loving.

By the way, if you are in a situation similar to the good girl above, you cannot help but castrate. It's what a normal human being does. You're a complex and powerful woman. If you just shrivel yourself up, what happens to all of that juice and joy of yours? It turns directly into castration, and good girls castrate so that it sticks. Their unhappiness broadcasts, and it stays inside their men like rusty hooks.

Tender issues

The good-girl approach will wipe both of you out. Your appetite is either satisfied, or your relationship dies. You should either get with the programme or get out. Luckily, The Training Cycle is the way to start putting yourself into action. Even so, your man may take a while to come around. With your new, confident sense of yourself, it's easy to get impatient. In a few cases, some women may be tempted to take him down a notch even in the midst of making love. We have to tell you, however, that this is a mistake. You get him interested, and now you're going to get-him-but-good? You will succeed, we guarantee it.

If you think his genitals are hanging by a thread at other times, just wait until sex. Castration is nowhere so close to literal as during lovemaking. You castrate him when he thinks he is being your hero lover, and he may never touch you again. Sure, he's got an inflated ego. But it flattens in a pop. Give him wins for anything you can find right, then let him know he's still a hero by giving him a problem to solve for you. When he does it, let him know he put a song in your soul, an orgasm in your heart, a smile on your lips.

So he's rubbing you as if you were made of shoe leather, and you want to break his hand. But you keep cool. You grab his arm, give him a kiss, and say, "I love you being attentive to me. Could you rub me lighter, honey? Yes. Even lighter than that. Yes. Much better. Even lighter than that. Yes. Perfect. You are such a great lover."

There may be times during sex that you want to cut his hands off, or even his penis, but the degree to which you avoid anger is the degree to which you will get what you want. This is not being a good girl. You're not embarrassedly shrivelling yourself up. You're just backing away from the anger. You have two major seducers, here — pleasure and anger. Stay with the pleasure. Stay with your appetite. He's just a dummy, after all. Some goof ball in high school told him that women love to have their nipples squeezed as hard as humanly possible, and for the last 25 years, he's been squeezing them with all the dutiful torque he can muster. And no woman has had the wherewithal to tell him that it hurts like hell.

This is even for those of you who think you have real dead-heads on your hands. You hear us say that all he wants to do is please you, and you mutter, "Oh yeah — sure he does." By now, you're not even sure you're interested in training him sexually. So let's get real, here. Here's a guy who is winning with you enough to hang around, but far from enough to be all over you with attention. Using The Training Cycle once is not going to change that. Nobody said it would. But if used repeatedly it will, because your man is wired up to win. He has no choice about it. If he finds that he is winning around you, you'll find that he is directing his attention your way. It's then up to you to keep him busy.

Where did the romance go?

In the beginning of your relationship, of course, you didn't have to perform any training nonsense at all. Everything was already hunky-dory. Every time your man even touched you he was winning. So where did the romance go?

Who knows? Scientists have suggested that change in

relationships is a biological thing. There is a chemical called *phenylethylamine*, which is supposed to be similar to cocaine, that the brain causes to be secreted at the first blush of love. This is new-romance chemical with all of its frenetic sexiness. As time goes on, however, the brain causes chemicals called *endorphins*, similar to morphine, to be secreted. So this is apparently long-term love with all its mellower pleasures. Scientists have even found a "cuddling" chemical involved in all this.

So if you really want to have the exact same experience you had early on in your relationship, either take cocaine (we're joking here), or take another lover (joking here, too, please). Besides, we are told that withdrawal from morphine is much tougher than from cocaine. Generally, people seem to prefer long-term relationship over short-term frenzy, though both are very nice.

But the chemical answer to love and relationships is silly. We don't care how many chemicals researchers can come up with, love and romance is dialogue, interaction, play, courtship, seduction, give and take, production, being swept off your feet and all the rest of it. After the scientists have completely alienated us from our bodies and our natural pleasures, they'll inject us all with chemicals to fill the void. When you were in love and romance, we bet you didn't think of "phenylethylamine" once. Identifying these chemicals is fine, but saying that they are the things that *constitute* love, sex and romance is false.

So let's take back the humanity a little. We need to let you know that much of your romance simply went the way of his not winning any more. That is, you've already been won. You are no longer the unconquered mountain. We know that sounds rather horrid, but it isn't. If you again supply the wins and the appetite ("Could you kiss me here?"), he'll be back in the game. If you want to put a little short-term frenzy back into the long-term, start inserting the wins and wants. Your native turn-on, sexiness and juiciness will take over soon enough. You'll both be back inside the instinctive validation of lovemaking and romance in no time. And all of those chemicals will take care of themselves.

A trial run-through

To get it started, and to end it up with future promise, The Training Cycle is the only way to go. Therefore, let's do a run-through. You will obviously make up your own words to fit your own style, but it's nice to feel your way through one example. So let's say you and your man are watching Tv.

You: I sure love you being here with me.
Him: Mmm.
You: Could you come over here and hold me for a little?
Him: Okay.
You: Thanks, honey. That's nice.
You: You are a great husband.
Him: What's got into you?
You: I just appreciate you.
Him: Well thanks. I appreciate you.
You: I just want to spend some time with you. Could you turn off the Tv for a while?
Him: I'm kind of interested in this show. (Don't back down, don't back down, don't back down)
You: Look — I think you are the best. I want to be with you quietly.
Him: (Sigh, grimace) All right.
You: Thank you, baby. I appreciate it. (Let's say he holds you again)
You: You smell good. Kiss me a little, okay?
Him: (Does it)
You: Wow. Mmm.
You: You are so sexy. Let's play around a little.
Him: Now?
You: Yeah. You're so great to be with. I want to be together in bed.
Him: Well, okay. Sure.
You: Thanks, honey.
You: (As you jump into bed) Yes! My man. Kiss me … You really turn me on. (Aside: Your natural sexy appetite kicks

in at different times on different days and probably with different wallpaper. But at some point, he will start responding more eagerly. For practice, however, let's continue with the dialogue.)

You: You are so spontaneous. I want to try something with you — can you do something with me?

Him: I guess so.

You: Good. I love that you are so willing. Could you take some of this and rub it between your fingers a little, and then rub me lightly with it?

Him: Where did you hear about this — one of your [magazines/ girlfriends/ secret lovers] ? (Aside: Production panic: he is formulating the doubt, "She doesn't like the way I make love to her.")

You: I read about it. It sounded fun. *I love the way you make love to me.* You're so attentive (or manly, or big, or fun, or strong, or smart, or sexy, or whatever is true for you. This is your money. All we're doing is running out one scenario).

You: Could you try it?

Him: Yeah, okay.

You: You're great.

You: Oh. That's good. Could you rub just a little lighter? Yes. Great.

You: You are really good. Could you go now with just a little bit more pressure? Perfect! Oooh.

You: You are so loving. Could you try it just a little higher? Yes.

You: Mmm. That feels great. Could you do it slower? Yes.

You: Honey, thank you. Could you go a little faster than that?

Him: I was rubbing you faster before.

You: You're doing great, baby. Could you just go a *little* faster? Yes. That's perfect.

You: (Pant, pant) That's wonderful. Try it in little circular moves for a second … Is that circular? Hmmm. It's okay, but I think I like back and forth better. Yes. Yes. Wow. Yes.

You: Yes. Keep going. Yes. Just like that. Oh baby. Oooooh.

And immediately you gain entrance to:

THE POWERFUL, SENSUAL SEXY-WOMAN HALL OF FAME
for brilliance, clarity and sparkling self-interest in finding your
man right as he produces for you the galactic star-shooter orgasm of the century.

Notice that every interchange above stays true to The Training
Cycle. Every interchange starts with a win which serves as the
fuel for your man to give you what you want. After the important
first win, you then give him a problem that he is able to solve.
And when he solves it, he's waiting to know if he did right, so
you give him the second win to close the cycle and build his
confidence as your producer-hero.

You don't need to turn this into a worrisome chore. Do
your own thing. If you initially manage only a single
win-problem-win interchange each day, that's fabulous. Try more
later. Nobody is looking over your shoulder. Our scenario just
shows how it might happen. You can fumble around, make
mistakes, mess it all up. Who cares? Just so you're having some
fun. But if you're interested in building up the confidence to go
past resistance and resentment to get what you want from your
man, then we suggest you start little dialogues like this one.
You see, we have more in store for you. How would you ever
be able to take advantage of it unless you train your man?

Chapter 15

More Sex

*Where you consider oral sex, fantasies, G-spot orgasm,
sexual "peaking", and increasing your level of sensuality*

You may not feel like training him to please you all the time, in which case you can certainly be the more active one, the one doing him and discovering what he wants. Since you're the instigator anyway, a more aggressive role can feel arousing and freeing. A dignified and noble way to initiate sex, for instance, is to reach over and start rubbing his penis. Even he will be able to understand this elegant approach.

When you want to be on the receiving end, however, it doesn't even have to be all fingers and lubricant. You can train him in oral sex, for instance. Cunnilingus is very popular among some men because they win so big with it. If you are embarrassed about having him do this, however, neither he nor you will have much fun. For many women, the embarrassment is just about their scent. This embarrassment goes away if they simply wash themselves thoroughly. You also may not like it if he is performing this the way another woman trained him. But if you love it, and he is winning, he will love it.

Magical incantations

Whether oral or digital, however, just remember those magical words from our last chapter: higher or lower, faster or slower, back-and-forth or circular, heavier or lighter, more to one side or more to the other side. Maybe one hand caressing your breasts, or some fingers of his free hand inside you. Or between the lips of your mouth. Another good one, obviously, is teasing. If you want the intense pleasure of that extended build-up, you have to slow him down and teach him to tease you.

So what have we stumbled onto? Communication in sex? What a concept. Conversation is sex; communication is sex. Monologue is rape, but dialogue is lovemaking. Start talking. Start during foreplay. Start saying what you feel like doing. Start asking him what he feels like doing. Start getting into dialogue. We know this is embarrassing, scary and strange, but do it. You now have the tools to pull it off successfully.

You're not the only one with the communication challenges, you know. On his side of the bed, every time he has ever been in dialogue with a woman, he has either been wooing someone he doesn't know, or he has been castrated with complaints and accusations from someone he does know. Since he happens to know you, guess which category you fall into? So tread lightly. In fact, for a while, we do not recommend communicating in sex other than with The Training Cycle. It establishes a very secure foundation. Eventually, he will realise he is winning with you, and you will be able to have more back-and-forth communication without his becoming paralysed.

Fantasy and acceptance

If you're stumped for sexy small talk, try a few fantasies. They're just a dandy way to break the ice ... sexually speaking. At the same time that we all have expectations to be connected, adoring and intimate in sex, we still have these human brains that buzz along all over the place. What's the buzz? Fantasies. Men and women fantasise the same amount, but both tend to remain very private about them. This may be because fantasies accompany the private affair of masturbation. Or it could be because some fantasies seem sick or weird. But fantasies are always and everywhere. Every time someone is attracted to someone else, sexual fantasies leap to the fore. These are the channels that are never turned off.

What's more, even "normal" people have had every fantasy you could ever come up with. The same-sex lover (even if you're heterosexual), the slave, the dog, the chains, the egg beater (?). Some women fantasise about sex with their daughters.

One man had an orgasm one night while dreaming of a frog jumping off its lily pad ... try to top that one. So these brains of ours are all over the place, and our fantasies come with the package. Fantasies do intensify sexual pleasure, but realise that fantasies are not reality — by definition.

Actually, the fantasy is usually better than reality. People can be disappointed when they try to act out a fantasy, because suddenly it isn't a fantasy any more! It used to provide a kind of mental focus for sex, but now it's gone, and all the other mental debris is bubbling to the surface during the most sacred of sexual moments. For this reason, some have recommended that fantasies remain secret. So if you opt not to share them with your man, at least be sure to use them. Your fantasies are projections of what you want. Look at them and see what you like, so that you can start training your man to produce similar kinds of experiences for you.

If your man is winning with you sexually, however, we recommend sharing. It's a great way to establish a new level of intimacy, and it validates wild, kinky, or embarrassing sides of you as being acceptable. You get to validate his fantasies as acceptable too, by the way. As such, it can allow each of you to talk a fantasy through during sex for the other person. This can be a lot of fun, because it moves the fantasy out of monologue into dialogue — where your relationship is.

Peaking

So now that we have paved your way to great intimacy, and orgasm after orgasm after orgasm, we're going to take it all cruelly away and offer something else. "Peaking". It's kind of like orgasm, but a whole lot longer. There is a bit of a trade-off with it: it's also not as intense. But you can keep your pleasure going and going, and all the time, your capacity for pleasure continues to expand. It's very simple. Have your partner bring you right up to the brink of the "Big O", then have him back off a little.

Peaking is the perfect addition to teasing. Remember those short, light, tantalising strokes that have you begging for more? These strokes will tumesce you quite effectively toward climax.

And then right at the edge of the big plunge, a series of longer, heavier, slower strokes will detumesce you away again. Your man can bring you up and bring you down, and bring you close, and take you away again. You can triple or quadruple your regular time before you orgasm (don't worry — you do get to orgasm), and all of this time will be pure pleasure. Pleasure which expands your capacity to experience even more pleasure next time.

As with teasing, peaking takes your attention off the big push for orgasm. We sometimes treat orgasm as if it's the last entry in our to-do list. After your partner "peaks" you a few times, you can tell him to bring you all the way to climax, so don't worry about that. But until that point, you can take more time to enjoy yourself. Some women report super-intense orgasms after repeated peakings, while others report about the same intensity. In either case, know that you'll get yours eventually. Until then, just how hot can you stand it?

Peaking is great training in the reverse, also. You can "do" him the same way he did you — fingers, lubricant, more pressure and The Training Cycle. Because he is now the one in the "appetite" role temporarily, this time *he* doth utter forth The Training Cycle to indicate what he wants. In any case, if he can trust you enough to let you take him up to, and away from, orgasm a few times, you have a man who can tolerate real pleasure. You've got a man with a slow hand. You've got a lover with an easy touch.

Yin-Gaſm

We promised earlier that we would also discuss the reputed G-spot. First of all, if you're not quite sure where this item is, it's located on the front wall of the inside of your vagina, about two inches above your clitoris. Your man can sometimes feel it with his finger as a small ribbed area, or sometimes as a smooth little circle, on the upper inside of you. But not always. So you are the prime locator. When your man puts a little pressure on it with his finger, you will probably detect it as a slight giggly sensation, or, because it is behind your urethra, one that makes you want to urinate. Even if you can't isolate it exactly, it doesn't matter that much, because it's usually all involved in your regular clitoral orgasm anyway. If you have no luck at all finding this area, by the way, you still don't need to worry. Some researchers claim that not all women have a single, isolated G-spot.

The G-spot is interesting mainly because it establishes at least a couple of types of orgasms, something which women have always claimed. The G-spot even seems to connect to different nerve pathways than the clitoris. However, although you might be able to experience an orgasm by having the G-spot massaged, don't expect the earth to move; it is much lighter than the clitoral orgasm you know. It seems to be a more nonlocalised, delicate sensation, as opposed to the concentrated orgasm of the clitoris. Women have described it as "more internal," "deeper," "fuller but not stronger," and "more subtle." Because it is generally a softer experience, some Tantra teachers have referred to it as a "yin-gasm", an orgasm of very feminine emotions and energy. For many, in fact, this area is not so much a sexual zone as it is an emotional zone. Rubbing this area seems to put a few women through an emotional process accessing variously sadness, anger, giggling or even sleepiness. A few women also ejaculate fluid during G-spot orgasm. The fluid is not urine, and it is not natural lubricating fluid. It is an odourless, light, non-sticky fluid similar to lukewarm water.

However, maybe 80 per cent of all women experience some combination of both kinds of orgasm anyway. One can try to separate one orgasm from the other, as researchers have done. But the most satisfying orgasms, as you would expect, tend to include both, whether your clitoris or your G-spot gets the most attention on the way there. So it's another one of the great wonders of women's bodies, but you don't have to pay much attention to it. We mention it because some women thought they were really missing out if they didn't have some version of this yin-gasm. Check it out some day, but don't sweat it.

Becoming full

At this point, we may be covering more about sex than you really wanted to know. If so, this is an example of what happens when your appetite is satisfied. It's called, appropriately enough, "getting full". No big mystery. You're eating a splendid French meal, the sauces are delicious, the wine is perfect, the entree tender and juicy. You are feeling wonderfully full. You know that if you take just one more bite, it will be too much, but it's so tasty, you just have to anyway. And it's too much.

We are sometimes so starved for a little pleasure that we gorge ourselves on it when it's here, as if it will never come our way again. We're not talking about hippopotamus gulps; those are appetite. This time, we're talking about stuffing ourselves. Since the only monitor of how full we are is our own feelings, it is essential we remain diligent. If we don't, we'll get sick. And for a long time after, we'll be repelled by whatever we over-indulged in.

The same concept applies to intimacy and relationship. Sometimes your man is just too much. He is around too much. Or maybe you've spent enough time together in bed, and you would like to get away for a bit. Constant sweetness in a long-term relationship often falls into this category. Too much niceness and sweetness! You start wanting to have a good fight, or whine and complain just so you can have a change of diet.

We bring up being full because recognising it is essential to sustaining pleasure, and not turning pleasure into the displeasure to which we are all accustomed. When you sense that taking the last little bite will put you over the top, gracefully back off. Give it a rest for a moment, or an hour, or a day, and rejuvenate your senses again.

Being full should therefore be part of the communication between you and your man. It's crisp and clean to make "full" an acceptable part of your vocabularies. If you are full of lying around with him, you don't have to do anyone any favours by lingering. Same with him. Chances are when he is full, you are too, so it's a relief to be able to communicate about it simply and safely.

Reach-Retreat

Fullness will make you feel like pushing him away. But the opposite end of the spectrum makes him want to push *you* away. We all know that your appetite can attract, but too much appetite — "neediness" — repels. If appetite attracts, why would it be that this "super-appetite" repels? Because feminine appetite is usually in a lovely state of balance where back-and-forth dialogue still resides, where give and take resides, where attraction is balanced by a little resistance.

But neediness is outside dialogue, beyond give and take. Neediness is all take. We would therefore like to introduce you to another law of the universe. Remember the first and second laws? *Pain brings forth more pain,* and *pleasure brings forth more pleasure.* This third law is no less important. It's called the law of *reach-retreat.*

When you ignore someone, for instance, it tends to bring that person around, whether it brings just his thoughts or also his body. Women have generally mastered this aspect of human communications better than men. When a man is attracted to a woman, she doesn't just throw herself at him. It isn't pleasurable to do that. Rather, the natural thing is to retreat a little. Which of course causes him to reach further and, say, ask for a date.

When that earlier woman stopped retreating from the fellow pursuing her and instead said, "All right ... but you'd better be good," she turned his "reaching" into an about-face. Well, the opposite also holds true. When you are reaching, when you feel you are intensely needing someone, that person tends to go away. When you reach, he retreats. If you then retreat, he reaches. This is an absolute law of the universe.

Maureen: *Needy Janie*

Janie thinks she needs success, independence, and the perfect body to make her happy. I've watched her work like a dog over the years, always aiming for the top in recognition and achievements — martial arts competitions, championship horse riding, whatever. I'm convinced that part of her sweet, meek, humble appearance comes from the fact that she thrives on struggle and pain.

Although I have known her for twenty years or more, I've

never known her to be in a happy relationship. The men drop like flies. Just recently, she was on vacation with a very nice gentleman she had known a few years before. He was recuperating from his break-up with a long-term relationship, and he invited her to spend a month vacationing with him.

With all of her struggle, Janie had not been nourishing her own needs and wants. She was therefore fixated on having sex with him. But she had not started off with the simple steps it takes to train a man to give her what she wanted. When Janie called me, therefore, she was upset because this man had not shown any desire for her at all.

I told her that it wasn't her attractiveness which was the issue. It was that he felt unable to perform up to par to satisfy her expectations. He felt pressured and uncomfortable around her — her "gradient" was too high. I told her to start taking care of herself immediately. When he is out for a while, take a long hot bath, rub and massage yourself tenderly, then wear some sexy clothing and take an hour or so to "do" yourself, I said.

That is, nourish herself by rubbing her body and bringing herself to orgasm. Take the edge off. She later reported that she did what I told her, and it worked. She felt so much more relaxed, and without consciously changing a thing, she suddenly started drawing his attention. Soon after, they made love, and what had been a rocky start for a vacation turned into a beautiful experience for both of them.

Viʃiting ∂ignitary

You can and should take care of yourself when needed. Doing it up right is a process called *visiting dignitary*. Pretend that you have an important dignitary visiting your bedroom tonight. You want everything to be perfect. Elegant. Beautiful. So you clean the room thoroughly. You make everything pretty. You get rid of the papers, books, television (and grubby sofa!). You polish surfaces. You arrange things attractively.

You bring in flowers and smooth, fresh linen, maybe attractive candles. You waft some special scent into the air. You bring food: grapes, peaches, strawberries, nice crackers and cheeses, maybe chocolate. Gooey foods are wholly appropriate. You include a soft, clean, dry towel and cloth napkins. You spend approximately three hours creating your pleasure palace. Too long? One woman claimed that this was the most powerful process she had performed in her entire life.

Why? Because it is a deep act of caring for yourself. For possibly the first time ever, you are the dignitary. You are the royalty. This is for you. Just how much do you care for yourself, anyway? Are you important, beautiful and feminine enough for three hours, or are you a rush job? Put your regular life on hold this one night. Tonight, you make sure you are far away from obligations and expectations. You take the phone off the hook. If you have an answering machine, you make sure you cannot hear it clicking if it engages calls. No deadlines tonight. Your to-do list is far away in a different life. A visiting dignitary is not to be bothered with such details.

You run water for a bath, and dissolve extra bath oil into the water. You have elegant soaps and shampoos available to you. You make sure the air is warm, so that you aren't chilled after bathing. You take your time during bathing. As you wash, you move slowly and gracefully. You appreciate your woman's body, its curves, smoothness and sensitivities. You massage areas that want it. Scratch areas that want it. Languish and enjoy.

After bathing and drying, you move into your bedroom where the clean sheets have been peeled back for you. Everything is just right. Everything is beautiful and sensuous. Candles are lit, lights are dimmed, you smell the delicate scent you put in the air. Your few luscious foods are near. You slip into bed feeling the crisp, fresh sheets against your skin.

Now you begin to appreciate yourself and your body. You can touch yourself lightly and teasingly. Face, backs of arms, breasts, nipples, inside of thighs. You may touch your genitals lightly or more deeply. Maybe you now switch and massage your scalp a little; then the back of your neck. Again, take your time. Eat a bit if you want, and wipe your hands clean with the towel.

If you feel like touching your genitals more, you rub some of that lubricant onto your fingers. You sensitively explore around and within. You sense the tissues near your clitoris; you feel your clitoris. You experiment: what arouses you, what brings you down from arousal, what feels best, what feels different. Light pressure, firmer pressure, quick, slow — you find what you like, and you let yourself have that. There is no hurry. You have the whole night.

When you feel like it, you start to take yourself to orgasm. Don't be reluctant to use more lubricant. You may first try peaking yourself a time or two, but whether you do or not, you still enjoy "the trip" in addition to the climax. Then you do whatever you want — keep experimenting, eat or sleep. Whatever you do, you continue to do it for you. You continue to care for yourself and love yourself. You care for yourself on a level that a pampered dignitary would expect.

Maureen: *Where everything starts*

Right after my divorce was a period of pain and loneliness. With four teenagers needing more attention and discipline than I could handle, I would often cry myself to sleep each night, missing my man and feeling extremely sorry for myself. I refused to talk to anyone about it, because I have zero tolerance for self-pity in others, and here I was wallowing in it. One night brushing my hair in the mirror, I looked at the tears welling up in my eyes, and I was disgusted. "That's it," I said. "I've had enough."

I remembered learning Visiting Dignitary in a workshop on sensuality. So the next day, I went out and bought a beautiful silk nightie, and I prepared my room with my favourite flowers, music and scent. I was devout: I did the entire process every night for a week, and I tell you, I was reborn. I hadn't slept so peacefully in a year and even had optimism and extra energy for working at my business. Most importantly, I was able to start dating men again. It transformed me. It transforms everyone, male or female.

We have heard claims of more energy, cured migraines, cured insomnia, peace of mind, more love, more turn-on in their relationships and less anger. Colours can even seem more vivid for a day or so. You are the appetite and source for sex. And you can give this to yourself whenever you want.

Chapter 16

Hexing and Communication

Where you discover the contents of a hex and the specific place for open communication

Reach-retreat explains why emotional neediness requires a little *pruning back* for dialogue, romance and seduction to have a chance. It is an important working principle of relationships, but it is also interesting in its own right. Because it is a *law*, you would expect it to make sense. Reach-*reach*, for instance, would make much more sense. If you reach he reaches, if you retreat he retreats, and both of you are as happy as sandboys.

But it doesn't work this way. Instead, reach-retreat is a clear contradiction. It explains a lot. For one, we can see the foundations developing for either the give-and-take of romance and seduction, or even a natural deviousness in relationships. In an extreme form, it explains jealousy. Jealousy always causes him to reach. It always rattles the cage. Jealousy wakes him up when nothing else will.

Maureen: *Natural manoeuvres*

One man I had just started dating gave me a clue about keeping our relationship alive by saying, "Don't fall in love with me, because I'm only good for about six weeks. Then I get bored." I laughed because at the time I also fell into that category. Jealousy is not the optimum way to run a relationship because it gets hectic coming up with artificial supports and "hooks". But I did learn that jealousy is a useful tool to re-ignite the fires every now and then.

José and I had actually been dating longer than six weeks when I noticed our excitement starting to plateau. He was driving me home one evening when it occurred to me to experiment. When we pulled up to a stop light, I slowly turned my head to look at the man in the next car. I consciously decided to flirt.

We were both excitable, reactive types who picked up on each other's moods. So when José talked to me, I answered only vaguely so he couldn't help but notice my attention was diverted. When he finally looked in the direction of my gaze, he showed instant signs of annoyance. I pretended I didn't know what he was talking about, but still remained fairly distant throughout the rest of the evening. It worked unbelievably. We made passionate love as if it were our first time together.

Women are generally quite familiar with jealousy. You notice that your man is listening intently to some other woman, giving her more attention than he's shown you for a while, and you feel the grip. Your stomach tightens, your pulse quickens, your breathing speeds up. It is fear of loss leaping to the fore as you sense him retreating from you. So you "reach" as coolly and gracefully as you can by sauntering over and including yourself. You reach again by later bringing up her name. Even if he admits he was attracted to her, at least he isn't retreating any more. He isn't holding back secrets from you, so you can relax a little.

Jealousy has an interesting structure. Your efforts to include yourself are efforts to get out of being "at effect", without control. But this at-effect feeling can also combine with the seduction you see taking place. Therefore, you can inadvertently find yourself excited.

Jealousy is like the dark step-sister of sexual turn-on, because it contains many of the same elements. As with José above, jealousy brings up a clear pain-pleasure choice for the person experiencing it — either feel the excitement, or feel the fear. Jealousy can therefore be a potential source of turn-on in your relationship, but because the choice between the pain or pleasure is rarely easy, jealousy can also be an extremely wild, out-of-control ride.

Maureen: *Exclusion*

This discussion reminds me of my instant dislike for a woman who was a friend of my boyfriend. The two had never been lovers. In fact, she was happily married and seemed to be a perfectly nice person. I was interested in my reaction to her, because my confidence as a woman is generally above average, and I even enjoy my man flirting from time to time. So why did I resent her so much?

I soul-searched this one by thinking through the times I became irritated with her. Then I hit on it: she was a master at excluding me. Each time Geoffrey and I would meet her, she would graciously greet us, but then turn her intense focus on him. She would even embrace him intimately and kiss him on the lips with an air of ownership that women only display with their own men. Then, though we had met many times before, she would always have to be reminded of my name.

It wasn't the flirting. It was her rude intruding into my territory and her immediate excluding of me. Intrusion and exclusion. I was not one bit included in her friendship with Geoffrey, even though she knew we were dating seriously. She was what I call a Queen Bee: she demanded all the attention without regard to any other woman.

Both Reach-Retreat and jealousy are based on something called "hexing". The primary hex in the human domain is what Maureen discussed above — the hex of *exclusion*. Excluding people is akin to "banishing" them, a common form of criminal punishment throughout history. It can take the form of ignoring, disowning or excluding someone from a social group or interaction. It's powerful. With only jealousy, Maureen seemed able to allow the "turn-on" aspect and avoid the "fear of loss" aspect. But with exclusion, it wasn't so easy. Hexing sounds a bit evil, and indeed it can be if used irresponsibly. So first master The Training Cycle. It is enough to bring almost any man around, and to make things as alive, juicy and productive as you could ever want.

Your man is probably just a dead-head, or a jerk, or a mummy's boy like most men. These are not tough cases. He may also be wonderful, so you won't even have to think about hexing. The Training Cycle will work like rocket fuel if your man is even slightly awake. But if you are still frustrated about a certain issue, hexing is a way to cut past defences, threats, even culture and ideology, to elicit a behaviour you want.

In reality, we are all hexed every day. If you are single, and you see lovers kissing in the park, you are probably going to be hexed. If you drive a 1968 banger, and you park next to a brand-new Mercedes, you'll be hexed as a matter of course. You may have a conversation with yourself to justify your car, like, "At least mine is paid for." But such a thought process just affirms the existence of the hex.

The main thing to know about a hex is that it eventually causes you to be "hexed into" the thing hexing you. If all your close friends have lovers, you eventually get one. If all your close friends drive expensive cars, you eventually upgrade. Being hexed is uncomfortable, but it's also motivating. A "dare" is a hex, in fact. It's a challenge. It motivates you because it makes something seem more possible to you while at the same time questioning your abilities. It is both winning and losing.

Verbal hexing

The kind of hexing we will discuss here is "verbal hexing" — you will be able to open up dialogue about sensitive subjects while all the time preserving your personal safety. It is also a way to get through to men of impenetrable ego or exceptional stupidity. Please remember something, however — verbal hexing is for the purpose of bringing your man closer to you, not for getting even with him. Hexing is a very loving thing to do in a relationship, because you agree to stay with your man as he experiences self-doubt.

The basis of hexing is that it disarms the automatic defensiveness of your man so that you can get through to him, without you being devastated in the process. Just like a dare, it achieves this by combining wins and losses, wins with criticisms. The win must be the truth, and the criticism must address an issue you specifically want to handle.

Remember criticism? The big "no-no"? The thing that castrates your man and turns your relationship into a loser? Well, in this one, very precise case, criticism is not a castration. This is how to do it: you give him a win, then you criticise. The criticism is not intended to castrate and injure. It is intended to initiate constructive dialogue about the issue criticised. It is intended only to point to *something more that can be done*.

> You are a great provider. Yet you don't want to take any time to enjoy your family.
> It feels so secure to be with you; too bad we don't have much fun any more.
> You are such a sexy man; it all seems to be wasted when we're together.

You can see how intense hexing could become. Therefore, notice that each criticism does not contradict the initial win. If you were to say to someone, "I like your shoes. Too bad they're for an old lady," you aren't hexing, you are *castrating*. But if you say instead, "I like your shoes. Too bad about that belt," now you are hexing. You are indicating something more that can be done. What happens with a loving hex is that your man usually appreciates hearing the truth. He will feel it isn't something he gets from others.

Getting a response

You are looking for a response on the order of, "What do you mean, we don't have fun?" With this, you will have initiated the simple dialogue you were seeking. But remember: *do not change directions here*. In other words, the moment you have his attention, don't go into your whining, complaining and castrating. You have made it safely to very tender ground. If you start dumping complaints and castrations one after another, you won't believe the damage that will be done, possibly to yourself as well. Keep your head, and keep delivering hexes in win-lose order only. In this case, for instance, you can say, "You are a good, responsible man. It just seems you've lost your spontaneity."

It's another reason to refrain from hexing except as a very last resort. You had better know how to keep your head and stick to the programme. Women have been doing versions of hexing for centuries, but it's been so entangled with direct castration that it has more often hurt than helped. So remember that your intention is to open up your relationship and initiate dialogue or change without getting beaten. This is the time to listen to him. Carefully listen and carefully consider his responses. If he continues to defend himself, or to show anger, continue to hex. *Don't get sucked into fighting back.* Keep your power, or the whole thing will go down the toilet. One way is to take his last defence, turn it into your next win, and express your hex this way:

Him: I do everything I can to be spontaneous — you're the one who isn't spontaneous.

You: I know you do everything you can to be spontaneous, and I appreciate it so much. But you seem tired all the time around me.

When he is no longer defending, attacking or arguing, switch gears gracefully into The Training Cycle. Give him another win, and this time, tell him something that you want. If he agrees to it, give him a closing win. You should therefore be a pro at The Training Cycle before you ever use hexing. You should know it backwards and forwards. Hexing is only going to be effective when your man knows what it's like to be a winner with you. A man who only loses with you will be too burned out to respond.

As mentioned, hexing is evidence of intense caring for someone. During courtship, for instance, when a woman throws a criticism at her pursuer, accompanying it with a fun smile, she brings him closer to her. Without the smile, the win, he stops cold. But with the smile, he is "winning-losing" with her — he is hexed with her. He starts to crawl out from underneath his self-isolating ego.

As it turns out, we can see that The Training Cycle itself is a hex. You give him that first win (remember — the one you were so reluctant to deliver?) and then you give him a problem to solve which initially *represents losing* to him. So you give him the win, then you give him the "lose". All the time that he is solving your problem, he is coming closer to you and paying you and your appetite serious attention. The hex is what brings him close.

Blessing him into abandonment

The opposite of hexing is called "blessing". Blessing sounds so much better, doesn't it? Fine, but it actually drives your man away from you. What is blessing? What is the opposite of first giving your man a win, then criticising him? Simple — first criticise, then give him a win. Blessing is very close to "Reaching", a little-girl syndrome. Your man is losing with you — you are unhappy or negative, then you find a little bubble of good feeling, and you tell him how wonderful he is.

Sounds nice, but it will drive him away. It will drive him off somewhere to find an appetite and a sense of reality. Imagine it with yourself. You know that a certain woman dislikes you, but she walks up to you at a party, smiles and says, "So nice to see you." First, the dislike, then the win — you will want to leave. By the way, if you *want* someone to go away from you, blessing them is classy and effective. First criticise, then compliment.

Honest communication

But whatever happened to honest communication? All these games and hexes and training cycles sound like they might be appropriate for immature relationships, but not relationships like yours. Well, if the "honest communication" in your relationship involves delivering your complaints to your man whenever you feel the urge, your honest communication will destroy that relationship.

Or if your honest communication involves him expressing his anger in your face whenever he feels the urge, he will destroy that relationship. So what precisely do you wish to get across? How wonderful your man is? And then what you want from him? And afterwards how great it is that he performed for you? If so, it seems that The Training Cycle is already honest.

Or would you like to communicate all the things you don't like? All that you would be risking is your man's staying with you, or possibly your physical safety. It's up to you, of course, but both hexing and The Training Cycle might allow honesty *and* safety. Having said this, however, we have to say that we do support honest communication of the type suggested.

Yet first you must acknowledge that the "honest communication" you may be thinking of is not exactly of the positive variety. Believe us, no woman who sincerely wants to give her man compliments and praise has any problem doing it. The honest communication being described here is the negative — the stuff you don't feel safe delivering. If you try to initiate this negative communication trusting only in your sincerity and your great need to get something off your chest, you are walking on the thinnest ice you can imagine.

So here is the bottom line on honest communication: it takes two to tango. You must have full and secure commitment from your man to engage in the back-and-forth nature of this communication before you ever dip your little toe into it. And you'd better be able to trust him. You want to complain to a hair-trigger killer who wins or loses only through you? Good luck. The issue is safety. How do you guarantee your safety and his safety when engaged in this kind of communication? The best answer we have found is the following.

Maureen: *The communication game*

I have often used a certain communication game developed by a friend of mine named Airic Lenardson in the early 1970s. I have used it to maintain harmony and honesty with my children and my relationships; I have even used it in the workplace. It has been the most valuable communication tool I've found since learning how to talk.

For instance, I know a divorced couple of 20 years who became friends again after this game. Prior to playing it, the ex-husband said it would be useless because his ex-wife would never listen without walking all over him. As it turns out, they went ahead and played the game, and he felt safe enough to communicate with her for the first time in over 30 years of knowing her.

He told her exactly why he was unhappy in the marriage, and why he left. She was astounded and relieved that he would finally tell her the answer to the question that had tormented her since he left 20 years before. Both agreed that, had this communication taken place back then, he may never have divorced her. I have used this game with my mate when asking for what I want sexually, as well as other things that require a sensitive ear. I find that my man never gets upset, and he can digest my requests easily.

On the other hand, some people have not played this game according to the rules and have purposely got out of line because it started to reveal things they wanted to hold onto: things like cheating, being a bully, being a victim, or lying. So it must be followed word for word. If it is not played accurately, everlasting hurt and anger can be created. Don't start unless you have players who are willing to abide by some simple rules. The first round usually needs some coaching and correcting, but this is the gist of it . . .

When one person talks, the other listens with the intention of duplicating the speaker's experience, just as if it were themselves in the speaker's shoes. He or she does not get to speak, reply, judge, or think of anything else other than what that person is talking about. The person speaking, on the other hand, may say anything he or she wants regardless of how stupid, bizarre or insensitive. Or how long it takes.

The listener duplicates without judging, commenting, gesturing, expressing emotion, making faces, or "going away" mentally. One person starts the game off by asking the other precisely this: "What do you feel like saying?" The person addressed says, "I feel like saying [such and such]". That is, saying anything that comes to mind. He or she could also say, "I don't feel like saying anything". In either case, this speaker ends by saying, "and that's what I felt like saying".

The listener now says precisely, "Thank you." Then they switch and the previous talker now plays the role of listener, again initiating the process with, "What do you feel like saying?" The game continues back and forth until both feel they have completed what they needed to say. Such a point will be obvious, because both people will probably say, "I don't feel like saying anything else right now."

It should now be obvious why the "honest communication" you always crave must occur within a structure like that outlined here. When you indulge in your honest communication off the cuff, it almost always ends up hurting, because there is no safe structure that ensures you will each be heard. Problems do need to be handled from time to time. And if hexing is not your cup of tea, this "feel like saying" can work if both participants agree to follow the rules.

One oft-cited benefit to this game is it clears up so many snags and frustrations that you and your man are very soon restored to loving sexual intimacy. But don't think that this communication game is going to replace The Training Cycle. You may be able to clear up personal or relational problems, but it generally isn't going to produce anything. It isn't going to turn him into your winning hero. Safety is important, but it doesn't feed the rest of that appetite of yours.

Above all, you are the appetite. You are the source. You should get what you want. Knowing that your wants drive the whole game is actually a relief. When you find this out, you will naturally grow in self-esteem, power and pleasure, and naturally at your own pace.

Chapter 17

Love and Inspiration

In these few chapters, we outline practical steps which can serve as instruction and incentive for you. With these guidelines, you will be able to explore that world of pleasure which awakens when you get what you want from your man. But precisely because we have been practical, we may have stumbled into the world of "how-to", that world of rules, work and burden.

If we have, we apologise. Then we remind you that nothing is going to work in your relationship unless you are pursuing your own pleasure. If you reach the point of working at it again, then the rest of what we have said will lose its meaning. It will be as grim and empty as every other how-to advice has been. And so in this chapter, your authors are going to move back into the spirit of the thing.

This "spirit" is the discovery that you are the source of appetite, love and progress in your relationship. And though many women consider being in the driver's seat freeing and exciting, others may feel it's a burden. That is, why do we just talk to *you* about your relationship? Why don't we talk to him instead, and make him change? Why does it feel as though it's all on you? You sit there with this information stacked on your shoulders like a bag of grain.

Escaping from the monologue

So as much as your authors' intentions are good, we realise you are left holding that bag. So this is why we have been so insistent on this idea of dialogue. You sitting there stupefied under the bag of grain, all the information, is just monologue. It doesn't go anywhere and it isn't any fun. Similarly, the other side of the coin, doing whatever we tell you to do, word for word, is also a monologue — no fun, because there is none of your own thinking translating what you have learned into *your* life.

So we want to reiterate the dialogue. We have said you are powerful, but not the type of power which means force or *heavy burden*. We hope instead that we have given you an idea of power that is lighter, freer, more pleasurable. Power which is not stuck in a lonely monologue of domination at one end, or a lonely monologue of submission at the other.

Instead, dialogue takes place in the play between you and your man. Dialogue is love and fun. It is the dynamic interaction between two people, the freedom and ease between two people. Put pleasure first, step over anger whenever possible, and expertly run your man for what you want. It all starts with wins and appetite, and ends with fun and production. Remember the pleasure. And remember that this information is only for you. If you don't have any fun with it, then it's no good. That's the acid test. If you begin to enjoy new pleasure in your life and relationships, you did it.

Action and spirit

Your wants are the source of the entire play of dialogue in your relationship. That's how you can return to the naturalness of following your own pleasure: you need do little more than be in touch with an appetite that is there anyway. Look to your own desires, and put them in dialogue with your man. At the same time, stay aware of some of the obstacles that might get in the way. Anger, for one. Or it may seem scary to go only for the good, only for enjoying life and expressing appetite. Maybe you can't imagine yourself being lucky enough to succeed.

Our answer is simply to be easy with it. Consider it, use it a little, enjoy it. Remember your own pleasure. And in the meantime, *risk a little*. Get into some of the practical stuff, the practice and behaviours. Try it out. Do The Training Cycle a few times. See how it goes. See what you come up with. Keep the sense of dialogue going.

Someone said that the purpose of ritual in religion is to accustom us to the spirit and truths of that religion. If we act it out enough, we start to grow in the meaning of the ritual, because we start physically to "live inside" the ritual. In fact, one study explored what most influenced people's beliefs. Groups of avowed racists were exposed to three different programmes. One group looked at pictures of suffering minorities and were given arguments about the destructiveness of racism. Another group was led in extensive imagination exercises and emotionally re-created the experience of being discriminated against. And a third group was paid five dollars a day to hand out anti-racist leaflets on the street. The result? Handing out leaflets had the most influence. Only when we physically act out an idea do we begin to live inside that idea. Only then do we begin to grasp its spirit and meaning.

So it is the practical application of The Training Cycle which leads to more abstract experiences like joy, freedom or power. "Give him a win, give him a problem he can solve, give him a win for solving it," can be nothing more than a dull instruction. But it blooms within you quickly when you put it into practice. It becomes a liberation. You find yourself wanting more of this good feeling, so you start doing it for the sheer joy of it. It's actually selfish, but it's the kind of selfishness that is a delight for everyone. As we have said before, selfish pleasure becomes naturally generous pleasure. So look to The Training Cycle as you would a ritual, a ritual which allows you to live inside the spirit of a joyful and graceful man-woman relationship.

Unstoppable love

The big bonus is that such spirit will come back to you. You naturally start to get what you want, of course. But others will also start to be easier with you. You will find yourself more and more in an accepting world. When we talk about "getting anything you want" (by enjoying not having it, then enjoying the process of getting it, and then enjoying having it), we're talking about the one thing that stays through all of it. The enjoyment. Enjoyment is joy, the experience of ease, lightness and love.

196

Once pursued directly, this enjoyment and love start to take over and run the show. They start to nourish you from the inside out.

When you are being nourished like this, you naturally pull away from the addictions you may have to anger. Why get stuck in that body-rush when you're feeling fine without it? So you start to experience a kind of "detachment" that a spiritual seeker might recognise. Not dead mental detachment — somehow watching yourself from behind your own eyeballs, like a zombie — but joyous detachment from the addictions of anger, fear and blame.

Pleasure — a spiritual call

When you are giving and generous by nature, when you've got so much that you don't know what to do with it, the energy moves from within you outward. Much less works its way back to "get to you". You start to put pleasure first without even thinking about it. You translate things that aren't working into things you want. If things do get tense, you have all the tools you ever need to move your situation to a winning one.

Everyone, male or female, has a whole mass of stresses, obsessions, problems, neuroses, knots, kinks and snags which get amplified in relationships. Such snags always want to tangle us up in criticism and old pain. But routing around in that stuff is a self-fulfilling prophecy. Old pain has a logic to it that is circular — it spirals us right back into it. It always proves its case. But pleasure ignores it. Pleasure is having too much fun to be tempted.

And as long as you are not tempted, you are still the initiator, still the instigator. You inspire; you call. Both of these happen to be purely spiritual practices. "To inspire" means to fill with spirit. And "to call" is the meaning of an ancient word, *gheue*. This word has evolved over the centuries into our English word, *God*. When you call, when you express the depth of your desire, you align yourself naturally with that which calls and inspires all of us.

So finally, though you may have least expected it, it's a

spiritual quest that we describe here. Instead of using God to justify pain, fear and anger, you can now start to find love, freedom, pleasure and positivity. When you don't think it feels right to go for pleasure, then do it for God. Do it for your spirit. Do it for love. Want God to speak to you? Put God first, as they say. When your generosity is overflowing and the world can't seem to get to you, you are putting love and God first. God is calling you to the love which allows you to love. Go for that good, go for that love, go for that pleasure.